# Total Heart Health for Women

Dr. Ed and Jo Beth Young
Dr. Michael Duncan and Dr. Richard Leachman

W PUBLISHING GROUP
A Division of Thomas Nelson Publishers
*Since 1798*

www.wpublishinggroup.com

Published by W Publishing Group, a Division of Thomas Nelson, Inc., P.O. Box 141000, Nashville, Tennessee 37214. Authors are represented by the literary agency of WordServe Literary Group, 2235 Ashwood Place, Highlands Ranch, Colorado 80129.

*W Publishing Group books may be purchased in bulk for educational, business, fund-raising, or sales promotional use. For information, please e-mail SpecialMarkets@ThomasNelson.com.*

Unless otherwise noted, when first names only appear, they are fictitious names for real people or for composites of real people. Identifying details have been changed to protect anonymity. Any resemblance is purely coincidental.

### Library of Congress Cataloging-in-Publication Data

Young, Ed
    Total heart health for women / Ed and Jo Beth Young, Michael Duncan, and Richard Leachman.
        p. cm.
    Includes bibliographical references.
    ISBN 0-8499-0012-3
    1. Heart diseases in women—Popular works. I. Young, Jo Beth. II. Duncan, Michael, M.D. III. Leachman, Richard. IV. Title.
RC672.Y68 2005
616.1'205'082—dc22                                                      2005022149

*Printed in the United States of America*

05 06 07 08 QW 9 8 7 6 5 4 3 2 1

# CONTENTS

Introduction: Woman to Woman      vii
*You can have a healthy heart lifestyle in 90 days!*

1. The Heart of the Matter      1
*It's your total heart, not just the parts, that matters.*

## Part 1: The Unique Beauty of a Woman's Heart

2. The Wonder of a Woman's Heart      13
*Your heart isn't on your sleeve; it's everywhere!*

3. What's So Special About Your Heart?      23
*It pumps blood just like a man's but is affected by different hormones.*

4. Your Heart Connection with God      33
*You have the same spiritual capacity as a man but a different concept of God.*

## Part 2: The Enemies of a Woman's Heart

5. Your Heart Is a Target      45
*God wants you to enjoy a rich, full life; but someone else has other plans.*

6. Heart Health—A Real Life-and-Death Matter      53
*If you're not heart savvy, "love handles" are just the tip of the iceberg.*

7. Resist the Assault on Your Spiritual Heart      63
*Turn from fear and resignation, and your life will light up with hope.*

8. Are You Eating to Live or Living to Eat?      75
*The path to a healthy physical heart goes through your stomach.*

9. Calories: Are They Friend or Foe?      87
*Achieving healthy energy balance is all about healthy calorie balance.*

10. Four Health Trends That Can Hurt Your Heart      97
*Just because "everybody's doing it" doesn't mean it's right for you.*

# Contents

11. Five Fears That Will Erode Your Faith     107
    *If you can trust God for anything, why can't you trust Him for everything?*

12. Unblocking the Flow to Your Spiritual Heart     117
    *Five areas where you may be in need of "spiritual angioplasty."*

## Part 3: The Ongoing Health of a Woman's Heart

13. Energy from the Proper Fuels     129
    *How to get more bounce in your step with less jiggle everywhere else.*

14. Adding Fire to Dietary Fuels     141
    *Cholesterol, fiber, vitamins, minerals—and what they mean in your daily diet.*

15. Spiritual Energy for Every Hour of the Day     151
    *Enjoy God as you never have before, no matter how tough your life is.*

16. Heart Exercise for Fun and Personal Profit     161
    *Careful planning and variety are the keys to your "energy-out" program.*

17. Are You Getting Daily Spiritual Workouts?     175
    *A healthy spiritual heart needs exercise as much as it needs fuel.*

18. Be Your Own Diet Guru     185
    *Which of today's flashy pop diets are best for you? None of them!*

19. Get Your Guidance from the Guardian of Your Heart     193
    *Which of today's pop psychologists should you follow? None of them!*

20. Are You Ready for the 90-Day Challenge?     201
    *Is "next Monday" a good time for you to start transforming your life?*

    Total Heart Health Journal     208

21. Physical Energy In: Menus and Recipes     211
    *Twenty-one days of easy, healthy weight-loss menus for you and your family.*

22. Spiritual Energy In: 90 Days with God's Word     235
    *Bible passages you can "feed on" during your 90-Day Challenge.*

    Notes     237

# INTRODUCTION
## Woman to Woman

You can have a healthy heart lifestyle
in 90 days!

**Jo Beth Young**

It was one of those delightful get-togethers for coffee and conversation. Six of us women were sitting around the family room catching up on one another's lives. You know how fun it is being with friends and being real.

But the topic that day wasn't much fun. We started talking about our everyday aches and pains and problems, and everyone had something to contribute. Concerns ranged from high blood pressure to lack of energy to "twinges in the hinges" to weight gain to feeling puny and depressed. These were the kinds of concerns we might share with our doctors. But we relished the empathy gained from sharing with good friends.

I left that day aware that we had voiced many of the common problems experienced by lots of women, perhaps including you. These issues can be physical, emotional, relational, spiritual, or any combination of the above. But they all cause pain and in some way threaten the lifestyle of health and fulfillment we all desire.

*Total Heart Health for Women* is a positive response to some of the health concerns I heard that day—the same kinds of concerns you share with your friends, your doctor, or your counselor. They are the same concerns my fellow authors deal with in the lives of people every day. But this book isn't just about the causes of puffiness, pains, excess pounds, and feeling puny; it's about getting healthy and staying healthy in your body and your soul—in other words, a total health lifestyle.

Let me tell you where this book comes from as it relates to Edwin and me.

We grew up together in Laurel, Mississippi, and were married on June 28, 1959. Along the way we have been blessed with three fine sons, their precious wives, and nine grandchildren.

But in 1988, something happened that threatened to shatter our wonderful life together. While working out on the stationary bike one day, Edwin suffered serious chest pains along with heaviness in his arms. You can imagine how frightened I was as we rushed him to the emergency room. Doctors discovered that Edwin's lateral anterior descending artery was blocked. In those moments I knew the anguish felt by so many women whose husbands have had a sudden heart attack. Thank God, open-heart surgery was not necessary as angioplasty successfully reopened the blocked artery.

## Our Lives Changed and So Can Yours!

That experience was a wake-up call for both of us. We realized that maintaining a healthy *physical* heart is as important as maintaining a healthy *spiritual* heart. Our lives changed. We began practicing the principles presented in this book and encouraging others to do so as well. We are so committed to Total Heart Health at our church, that we have a worship center, a fully equipped fitness center, and a café serving healthy meals—all under the same roof!

I can say with confidence that if you implement the principles presented in these pages, your life will be changed as well! Edwin and I are living proof, as are hundreds of women in our church and community who have adopted the Total Heart Health lifestyle. We will show you how to replace bad health habits with a good health lifestyle in 90 days. This Total Heart Health lifestyle will transform you inside and out, heart and soul. It's our 90-Day Challenge to you.

Edwin and I have teamed up with two of America's top cardiologists to write this book. Rick Leachman has important insights into women's hearts, not just as a cardiologist but because he has a wife and two daughters. Rick and Marcy are active lay leaders at our church. In addition to English, Rick is fluent in Spanish and Italian. He sometimes needs to speak multiple languages as a cardiologist in the huge Texas Medical Center in Houston.

That's also where you'll find Mike Duncan, if you can catch him between surgeries and consultations. Mike studied under Dr. Michael DeBakey and Dr. Denton Cooley, two of the world's most famous heart specialists. Mike has special interest in surgical procedures for correcting hearts that are beating out of rhythm and for dealing with aortic aneurysms. Mike and his wife, Patsy, devote many volunteer hours to the church's medical team.

In this book, you'll also meet an impressive young woman, Kristy Brown. She is the physical fitness director at the Family Life Center of Second Baptist Church. Kristy graduated from college with a major in health and physical fitness, and she is certified by the American College of Sports Medicine, the Cooper Institute for Aerobic Research, and the Aerobics and Fitness Association of America, among others. Kristy wrote chapter 16, which focuses on exercise.

Most important, Rick, Mike, Kristy, Edwin, and I are students of the Bible. We all believe that to have Total Heart Health, you must take care of the total heart—spiritual and physical.

## A Recipe for Total Heart Health

I compare the 90-Day Challenge that we present here to the process of making bread—a lost culinary art in many of our homes. There are three stages to the process: sifting, kneading, and baking. Similarly, we see three stages of the Total Heart Health transformation, achieved approximately at 21 days, 45 days, and finally 90 days.

### Sift the Ingredients

First, you sift the ingredients together to remove the coarser elements and to create a new mixture for the bread you want to make. *The first three weeks of the Total Heart Health plan will help you sift out old unhealthy habits and replace them with new healthy habits.* For example, implementing our dietary recommendations will help you establish healthy patterns for eating the right foods in the right quantities. You will also be prompted to get into a program of daily exercise. And if a hectic daily life has left you feeling spiritually empty, you will begin carving out time to connect with God.

Many behavioral experts claim that it takes twenty-one days of repetition to break one habit and establish another one. After about three weeks of practicing healthy physical and spiritual disciplines, you should sense that you have established a positive, healthy new "groove" for your life.

## Knead the Dough

Second in the bread-making process, you knead the dough. Kneading by hand is hard work—repeatedly pressing, squeezing, and twisting your ingredients into an entirely new entity: bread dough. *During the next three to four weeks of the Total Heart Health challenge, you will fine-tune and feel more comfortable with the good habits you have established.* Sure, it will take a little discipline, but you're worth it!

If you're like many others who have stayed with our recommendations, about halfway through the 90-Day Challenge, your daily health disciplines will take on new meaning to you. You will sense a closer, more personal connection with God. Your outlook on life will be much brighter. And you will probably feel better physically and weigh a little less. Think of how encouraged you will feel! Just keep up the beat; you're still in the middle of a life-changing process.

## Bake the Bread

Third, you bake the bread. Peering through the oven window as the timer ticks away, you delight to see the loaf rising and turning golden brown. It's the finished product of your labor, and you can't wait to share it with family or friends. *During the second half of the 90-Day Challenge, you will look and feel more like the person you want to be than the person you were.* The healthy habits you have established become your normal, second-nature way of doing things. You no longer dread exercise; instead, you really miss that thirty-minute walk or jog each day when something unexpected cuts into your schedule. You don't think twice about passing up second helpings or a decadent dessert at the buffet table. And you find that among your first waking thoughts is the desire to enrich your soul by reading something from the Bible and talking to God through personal, heartfelt prayer.

## Our 90-Day Challenge to You

*We firmly believe that three months after embracing our Total Heart Health challenge, you will look into the mirror and see a new woman!* Why am I so confident? Because a lifestyle transformation has been the joyous experience of a rapidly growing number of women who have taken this challenge to heart.

The first step on the rewarding journey is to finish reading this book. These pages are filled with proven principles and helpful examples for both physical and spiritual heart health. Block out some serious reading time during the next week or so to work through what Edwin, Mike, Rick, Kristy, and I have to share.

The next step is to accept our 90-Day Challenge and begin your personal 90-day lifestyle transformation. We will give you the details on the 90-Day Challenge in the chapters ahead, culminating in chapter 22. To help you follow through with the challenge, I invite you to enter into a Lifestyle Transformation Commitment. You will find the form on page xiii. You may complete the agreement at any time between today and the day you begin your 90-Day Challenge.

Edwin and I have found that in order to make a significant change in our lives, we must make a serious commitment to change. Signing a commitment helps us follow through with the intentions of our hearts. That's why we encourage you to do so. Please note that signing your name on the 90-Day Challenge commitment expresses your *intention* to change. You may not reach all your goals or fulfill all your hopes, but your serious commitment will head you in the right direction. Making your commitment in writing will provide added momentum to complete the challenge.

Our approach to the disciplines of a healthy heart may seem legalistic to some. But there's a big difference between legalism and discipline. A legalist will try to follow every rule, trying to please the people she looks up to, including God. A disciplined person will bend every effort and make sacrifices to reach her desired goals. Legalism is not a healthy lifestyle, but discipline is. Discipline and self-control go hand in hand. No one can make a lifestyle change without exercising discipline, and that's what our plan will help you do.

Are you ready for a healthier heart? Then let's get started!

# Keys to Total Heart Health

## Introduction: Woman to Woman

- In 21 days you can begin to walk through life free of habits that threaten your heart health.
- In 40 days you can pick up the pace through new practices that will lead to improved heart health.
- *In 90 days you can be soaring in a brand-new Total Heart Health lifestyle.*
- We encourage you to prove to yourself that the Total Heart Health lifestyle works for you by trying it for one week.
- Daily, spend 30 minutes in personal time with God and His Word (see pages 235–36 for a list of Scriptures for personal study and meditation).
- Give another 30 minutes for physical exercise (see Chapter 16 for exercise ideas).
- Eat a sound diet throughout the day (suggested menus are found beginning on page 214).
- Don't wait for tomorrow. Take your first steps toward Total Heart Health today by reading on. In 90 days, you could be far down the road toward Total Heart Health!

# Total Heart Health

### Lifestyle Transformation Commitment

## 1. Your Personal Information

Name _____ Age _____

My present weight is _____.

My present body mass index (see chapter 8) is _____.

My present blood pressure is _____.

I presently spend _____ minutes per day in some form of exercise.

I presently spend _____ minutes per day in Bible reading and prayer.

## 2. Your Goals

In general terms, what do you want to accomplish by taking the 90-Day Total Heart Health Challenge?

_____

_____

_____

In 90 days . . .

I want my weight to be _____.

I want my body mass index to be _____.

I want my blood pressure to be _____.

I want to be spending 30 minutes per day exercising.

I want to be spending 30 minutes per day in Bible reading and prayer.

## 3. Your Commitment

Seal your agreement in prayer to God. You may want to pray the following prayer or use it as a pattern for your own prayer.

> *Dear Father, thank You for the heart You have given me. I now commit to pursuing Total Heart Health for the next 90 days. Give me the discipline and encouragement to live out my commitment. Develop in me a new lifestyle that will bring greater health to my total heart so I may fulfill the purposes for which You put me in the world. In Jesus's name, amen.*

Your signature _____

Date _____

# 1

# The Heart of the Matter

It's your total heart,
not just the parts, that matters.

**Ed and Jo Beth Young**

---

Carolyn is the envy of the lakeshore where she runs five or six mornings a week. When she glides by, glistening bronze sculpture in motion, heads turn. She's trim, toned, tan, and twenty-eight. Less-sculpted women look at Carolyn and say, "She wears spandex to show off what she's got; I wear it to hold everything in."

Fitness is more than a hobby with Carolyn; it's her career. Having earned degrees in business and health, she owns a small, upscale fitness club in the city and teaches classes in cardiovascular health and nutrition. Carolyn makes very good money, allowing her to afford a nanny for her preschool twins. And with the little boys taken care of, she constantly pushes herself physically—running farther and faster, working out strenuously, expanding the limits of her endurance.

What no one knows about this fitness goddess is that she wakes up in a cold sweat several nights a week, heart palpitating, stomach in knots, struggling to breathe. Carolyn has never lacked for male companions. But they all leave her eventually, just as Brett left their marriage two years ago. She feels so alone. Her heart aches for someone to love her for who she is, not just for her hard-body looks.

And for all the good Carolyn's focused diet and exercise are doing her physically, she feels empty at the core, as if her spiritual muscles are atrophied and useless. It's an even deeper ache than her desire for human connection.

Angie, a fifty-something wife and mother of three teens, lives in a world vastly different from Carolyn's. Most members of the small church Angie attends see her as a sterling example of spiritual and moral strength. Angie is usually the first volunteer for service projects. And when she's not spearhead-ing a project, Angie is just there for people in the church, especially the women—listening to their problems, praying with them, and sending encour-aging notes and e-mails.

Angie is so busy with church and family that she doesn't have time to keep herself in shape. Nutrition and exercise just aren't on her agenda. The meals she plans for the family—and eats herself—are quick, tasty, abundant, and loaded with calories, carbs, and fat. As a result, Angie is overweight by forty-five pounds—and counting. She can't walk up a flight of stairs without pausing to rest halfway.

Then there's Rebecca, who could be the poster girl for women who aspire to succeed as working wives and mothers. In grad school, Rebecca—a law student—met and married Carlos. Four years into her law practice, Rebecca gave birth to their first child. Rebecca and Carlos decided together not to give up Rebecca's career in order to be a stay-at-home mom. So after a short maternity leave, Rebecca was back in the office, often with baby and diaper bag in tow.

Cynthia is four now. Rebecca and Carlos have a fine-tuned schedule for tag-team childcare, which allows them both to keep working full-time with-out relegating Cynthia to day-care centers. On Saturdays, either Rebecca or her husband spends a few hours at work just to stay ahead. The six-day rou-tine is grueling and exhausting, leaving time for little else. But Rebecca is intent on achieving junior partner by the time she's forty, and Carlos is com-mitted to helping her do it. The couple is just as determined that Cynthia, the joy of their hearts, will not be a casualty of their career pursuits.

But there have been casualties from Rebecca's drive for success as a lawyer and mother. Her once-fervent faith in God has grown cold. A demanding schedule pushes Bible reading and prayer to the bottom of her daily to-do list, and they rarely happen. Sunday is kickback day for the family each week, and Rebecca guards the day fiercely. Church attendance has been jettisoned in favor of leisurely outings with Carlos and Cynthia.

Rebecca is proud of her accomplishments as a wife, mother, and profes-sional woman. But she senses that her life is out of balance, like a chair with four legs of different lengths. She would feel better about herself if she were more spiritual, but there is so much else in her life that needs her attention.

## Hearts Divided

You don't know these three women, but you probably know women like them. In fact, you may see something of yourself in these brief cameos of Carolyn, Angie, and Rebecca. Edwin and I have met many women like them wherever we have lived.

Busy lives, segmented lives, fragmented lives—they seem to be a sign of the times, don't they? There are so many demands on our schedules, so many tasks requiring our attention and energy. How can we put our hearts into everything? There just aren't enough hours in the day, and we don't seem to have the energy for all we need to do.

In a way, we're all composites of the three women above. Like Rebecca, about 60 percent of today's women work outside the home.[1] Add to the work-week a woman's activities with friends, activities at church, community service projects, and the endless list of chores around the house. Plus, we all have family responsibilities of some kind.

Then there is the side of life Carolyn represents. Who doesn't want to out-run the ever-encroaching pounds and expanding dress sizes? Who really enjoys getting winded in the first minute of a game of driveway basketball with the kids? In a perfect world, we would all still fit into our prom dresses when attending our twenty-fifth high-school reunions—and have the stamina to dance and party like teenagers. But for many of us in the real world, the tread-mill and our prom gowns were sold in a garage sale years ago, and the battle against calories, cholesterol, and pounds is a depressing standoff at best.

No wonder women like Carolyn, Angie, and Rebecca tend to live with hearts divided. Better to have it together in one or two key areas than to flounder in everything, they reason. Segmented lives and fragmented lives are all too common among the women we know. But it doesn't have to be this way, nor should it be. You are not a collection of parts that operate independently of one another. God created you to be a whole person with many closely integrated facets such as body, mind, emotions, and relationships. These areas are all interrelated and cannot be parceled out into categories of success or failure. When one area of your life is neglected or stressed, the whole person suffers as a result. A divided heart is often a hurting heart.

We want women like Carolyn, Angie, and Rebecca—and you—to grasp the importance of living wholeheartedly. When it comes to a woman's heart, the heart of the matter is the *total* heart. We believe God designed us to experience wholeness and health in body, soul, and spirit.

We're not saying you need to become some kind of Wonder Woman, such as a combination of Carolyn, Angie, and Rebecca. But you may be aware of areas of your life where you would like to enjoy greater health physically, spiritually, and emotionally. You might want to lose a few pounds and keep them off this time. Maybe you want to draw closer to God. Or perhaps you're just longing for your life to come together in all areas, to feel your heart is whole, together, and heading in the right direction. If so, this book is for you.

We confidently make you this promise: if you will devote about one hour a day toward Total Heart Health for 90 days straight—roughly thirty minutes to strengthening your physical heart and thirty minutes to strengthening your spiritual heart, along with a sensible diet—your life will be changed. You will begin to enjoy benefits that will last you a lifetime. We'll show you how to get started on the 90-Day Challenge, which will launch you into that healthy new lifestyle.

## An Undivided Heart

When I (Edwin) think of the journey of Total Heart Health, I am reminded of one of King David's prayers: "Put me together, one heart and mind; then, undivided, I'll worship in joyful fear" (Psalm 86:11 MSG). David apparently knew about the fragmented life and its pain. He cried out for God to pull all the pieces together so his total heart would be centered on God.

That's a great prayer, isn't it? "Lord, give me a whole heart focused on You." It so happens that such a prayer is completely in harmony with what God wants to do in every woman's heart. When you ask God for an undivided heart, get ready. That's just what He loves to do.

What will you discover on the road to Total Heart Health? Here are four important characteristics of the journey ahead.

## The Health of Your Physical Heart Is Linked to the Health of Your Spiritual Heart

Our culture is very health conscious these days. Just take a stroll down the health aisle in your local bookstore and see the myriad resources on every facet of diet and exercise. Seemingly every week, a new TV infomercial is touting another calorie-busting weight-loss scheme, fat-burning workout video, or ab-building apparatus made of chrome and plastic. It's all geared to help your physical heart tick stronger and longer—and make piles of money for entrepreneurs who trade on society's obsession with the perfect body. You could lose ten pounds just thumbing through all the weight-loss books!

But there is more to us than bones, muscles, and tissue. In the Bible, the creation account says, "The LORD God formed man of dust from the ground." That's the material, physical part of us, but God wasn't finished. The verse continues, "and breathed into his nostrils the breath of life; and man became a living being" (Genesis 2:7). "Being" in this verse literally means "soul." That's the immaterial, spiritual part of us—our thoughts, feelings, motives, choices, desires, fears, hopes, ideas, dreams, purposes, guilts, joys, and so on. And since the first woman was fashioned from the first man (see Genesis 2:18–23), we know women are made of the same stuff. But most men would agree that it's arranged much better.

God created us as whole persons with both physical and spiritual properties. We are physical *and* spiritual beings, and whatever happens to one part affects the other. No wonder the apostle Paul prayed, "May God himself, the God who makes everything holy and whole . . . put you together—spirit, soul, and body—and keep you fit for the coming of our Master, Jesus Christ" (1 Thessalonians 5:23 MSG).

God wants you to grow in health as a whole person. Physical heart health and spiritual heart health are tightly interlocked.

## Gaining Total Heart Health Is a Process, Just as Losing It Is

Having steadily gained weight for ten to twelve years, Jenny knew she had to make some changes to improve her health. She acknowledged that exercise was as important as diet in controlling her weight, but she was not athletic

5

and felt uncomfortable going into a gym. Developing a regular exercise program seemed an insurmountable challenge.

Then Jenny's brother gave her a membership to a private gym. Since she didn't want to waste his money, Jenny started forcing herself to go to the gym two or three times a week, early in the morning. At first, everything in her body and soul resisted working out. But after a month, it wasn't as difficult. And after three months, Jenny was actually looking forward to her aerobics class and her personal workout regimen. Her eating patterns changed, too, and she lost thirty pounds. She also noted improvement in her chronically high blood pressure.

Getting out of shape physically and spiritually happens over a period of weeks and months, so getting back in shape will take time too. Changing an unhealthy behavior pattern is nothing more than replacing it with a healthy behavior pattern. In the pages ahead, we will encourage you and coach you in the process of replacing unhealthy patterns with healthy patterns on the road to Total Heart Health—body and soul. This is no fad program guaranteeing instant success. It's a process in which every small step takes you farther from where you've been and nearer to where you want to be.

## Total Heart Health Involves the Spiritual Heart and the Physical Heart

In this book, we address the health needs of the physical heart and the spiritual heart simultaneously. You will notice at the beginning of each chapter one or two symbols, which indicate the emphasis of that chapter. Chapters marked with the symbol below on the left focus more on the spiritual heart. Chapters marked with the symbol on the right emphasize physical heart health. And chapters marked with both symbols below are intersections of the physical heart and the spiritual heart.

**Spiritual Heart**     **Physical Heart**

Your spiritual heart will strengthen as you devote some time each day to reading the Bible and praying to God. Jo Beth and I will take the lead in helping you strengthen your spiritual heart.

As a young man, I dreamed of building bridges, so I enrolled at the University of Alabama to become an engineer. But as a freshman, my belief in God was challenged by an atheist, so I launched into a serious search for God's purpose for my life. Six months later I committed my life to being a pastor, and I've been at it ever since.

Jo Beth and I have been a team for almost half a century. In addition to being a wonderful wife, homemaker, and mother of our three grown sons, Jo Beth is a Bible teacher and women's speaker. She is also an accomplished artist whose paintings reflect the joy and peace she imparts to those who know her. We want to share with you biblical principles and strategies to help you grow a healthy spiritual heart.

You will strengthen your physical heart as you take care to exercise each day and maintain a healthy diet. Mike Duncan and Rick Leachman will be the point persons on the physical heart track. They have extensive clinical experience and insight into women's heart health. They will share with you from their vast knowledge and expertise how to pursue and achieve physical heart health.

As you pursue these two tracks simultaneously, beginning with the 90-Day Challenge, your total heart will grow strong and remain strong.

## Total Heart Health Is Not a Fleeting Fad but a Lifelong Pursuit

The Bible teaches paradoxically that the total health of your spiritual heart will not be realized until your physical heart stops beating. For the Christian, death is the doorway into the fullness of life. So our spiritual heart health is always in process until we enter God's presence in heaven. As long as you pursue a deeper, more intimate relationship with God and His Word, your spiritual heart will improve in health.

As for your physical heart, you can look forward to a process of improving heart health over time—up to a point. But inevitably, age and perhaps disease or injury will weaken your heart, and it will stop beating for good. But in the meantime, you can and should pursue optimum heart health, both to extend and to enjoy the decades ahead.

This side of heaven, there is no point at which you can say, "I have arrived. My heart is totally healthy." There are always additional steps to take on this journey to maintain the level of heart health you have achieved and to lift your health to the next level. And every step you take is a positive step in the direction of Total Heart Health.

In part 1, we will explore the unique nature of a woman's total heart and why it is so important to pursue Total Heart Health. In part 2, we will unmask and disarm the deadly enemies of a woman's heart, those forces that can rob you of your health and even your life. And in part 3, we will look at numerous strategies for nurturing your total heart to constantly improve your health.

Here's to your health!

# Keys to Total Heart Health
## Chapter 1: The Heart of the Matter

- Segmented, fragmented lives are all too common among women today.
- God created you to be a whole person in body, soul, and spirit; and when one area of your life is neglected or stressed, the whole person suffers.
- If you will devote about one hour per day toward Total Heart Health for 90 days straight, your life will be changed.
- There are four important characteristics of the journey toward Total Heart Health:

  1. The health of your physical heart is linked to the health of your spiritual heart.

  2. Gaining Total Heart Health is a process, just as losing it is.

  3. Total Heart Health involves the spiritual heart and the physical heart.

  4. Total Heart Health is not a fleeting fad but a lifelong pursuit.

# Part One

---

## The Unique Beauty
## of a Woman's Heart

## 2
# The Wonder of a Woman's Heart

Your heart isn't on your sleeve;
it's everywhere!
**Ed and Jo Beth Young**

It has been a long and painful two years for Simone and Roland, the most severe test of faith and courage in their thirty-one years of marriage. Life is just beginning to feel refreshingly normal again. They can look forward to planning their tomorrows after months of merely trying to survive today.

It all started with the death of their only child, Chad, who was killed at age twenty-six in a fiery car crash. Both parents mourned the loss of their son, but Simone was overwhelmed by a sense of utter devastation. Grief and hopelessness hung over her like a gray veil for months. She vented her tearful anger at God as her trust in Him teetered in the balance.

Simone was just emerging from her deep grief when another blow put her on her back—literally. One day, while working in an inner-city kitchen serving lunch to the homeless, she suddenly felt nauseous and faint. Helped to a chair to sit down, Simone uttered the somber words that sent the other kitchen workers scrambling for the telephone: "chest pains." In less than twenty-four hours, Simone was being wheeled into an operating room for bypass surgery.

"You could have died in that kitchen, Simone." That was the opinion of the cardiovascular surgeon who skillfully repaired her damaged heart. Simone and Roland were stunned and deeply grateful that she had narrowly avoided a fatal heart attack.

"You may not be so lucky next time," the surgeon continued soberly. "And you will face this threat again unless you make some changes in how you take care of that heart of yours." Turning to her husband, he added, "That goes for you, too, Roland."

As you might expect, the couple was highly motivated to respond positively to the surgeon's admonition. Through the long months of Simone's recovery, they radically changed their lives. Roland scaled back his work at the company where he served as CFO in order to spend more time at home. He took the lead in studying nutrition, creating weekly menus of healthy foods and portions, and making sure they stuck to the diet. And as Simone worked her way into a regimen of daily exercise, she encouraged Roland to participate with her, so he did.

During their gradually lengthening walks together, the couple often talked about Chad. They cried together as they verbalized their deep feelings of sadness and loss, and they reminisced with laughter about the good times with their son. It was ironic, they agreed, that they may never have reached this stage of healing over their son had Simone's near-fatal heart problem not surfaced.

Simone and Roland also used this time to reconnect with God. Walking hand in hand, they began praying aloud together, something they had rarely done before. They tearfully thanked God for beginning to heal their hearts—physically, spiritually, and emotionally.

Today, the second anniversary of Chad's death, Roland walks into the house from work holding a large manila envelope with a big bow taped to it. Sitting at the breakfast table this morning, they had shed tears once more as they again thanked God together for their son, his all-too-short life, and the prospect of seeing him in heaven someday. But this evening Roland has a broad grin on his face as he hands the envelope to Simone.

"God has given us a new lease on life, honey," he says as Simone carefully opens the envelope and pulls out its contents. "And along with the good changes we've made, I want us to make one more. We have always talked about doing some traveling when I retire—you know, our dream of visiting the seven natural wonders of the world."

"Roland, what is this?" Simone asks, her eyes widening as she spreads out the brochures on the kitchen table: the northern lights in Alaska, Rio de Janeiro's fabulous harbor, the Great Barrier Reef in Australia, and Arizona's majestic Grand Canyon.

"Well, I can't wait until retirement," Roland continues with a laugh. "I cashed in a couple of healthy stock options today, and I'm going to start taking those weeks of vacation I've ignored. We need more than the right number of calories and carbs and proper exercise for healthy hearts. We need God and each other—and we need a vacation!"

## The Joy of a Healthy Physical Heart

It's wonderful to hear about heart-attack survivors, especially when they gain a new perspective of health that encompasses the total heart. And I suppose if we had survived what Simone and Roland survived, Jo Beth and I would want to enjoy a trip as well.

But we might have to debate with Simone and her husband over what is the greatest natural wonder in the world. I don't believe you have to leave the country or even your own community to experience the greatest wonder of God's natural creation. You don't even have to walk outside the door of your house. You need look no farther than your own body and the physical organ that keeps it alive—your heart. I would advocate to Simone and Roland and anyone else that the greatest natural wonder in God's created world is the human heart.

Throughout this book, Drs. Duncan and Leachman will tell you more about the wonders of your physical heart and the importance of keeping it healthy. But allow Jo Beth and me to give you a quick overview of your own heart in nontechnical terms.

Make a fist with one of your hands, right there where you're sitting; then take a good look at it. Located somewhere behind your ribs in the middle of your chest, your heart is about the size of that fist. Every minute of your life, at least a gallon and a half of your blood is pumped through your heart. And when you're running up the steps or playing a game of tennis, it can pump up to eight gallons per minute through about sixty thousand miles of arteries, veins, and capillaries. Amazing!

You may have been told that your heart keeps up this pace for a lifetime without any rest. Technically, that's not true. You've heard a human heartbeat amplified, haven't you—if not your own, perhaps the heartbeat of a loved one?

To me it sounds like the heart is saying, *Loved up, loved up, loved up, loved up*—which is a good thing for a heart to say. But between every *up* and the next *loved* is a pause that's about twice as long as the beat. God masterfully designed your heart with a built-in R&R feature. It rests and relaxes between every single beat. No wonder it can keep ticking for eighty, ninety, one hundred years or more.

I believe God's design for your heart tells us something about His design for the rhythm of our lives. We need to rest and relax twice as long as we work. And isn't it interesting that the common workday is about eight hours and that we use about twice that amount for sleep and recreation? When people stray from God's rhythm for work and rest—I'm talking about workaholics here—they add undue stress to their hearts, and that can lead to all kinds of physical problems.

Here's another fascinating fact about your physical heart. It has a built-in pacemaker that keeps it ticking like a watch connected to a hundred-year battery. About seventy to eighty times every minute, an electrochemical charge sweeps over your heart, and it beats in response to this charge—*loved up, loved up, loved up*. Even more interesting, this pacemaker of yours is self-generating. You cut the nerves to your legs, and they won't move. You cut the nerves to your lungs, and you stop breathing. But if you cut the nerves to the heart's pacemaker, it will keep on zapping the heart with that vital electrochemical charge. It's like the Energizer Bunny!

As magnificent and efficient as your heart is, your heart isn't what keeps you alive. It's what your heart delivers to the cells of your body that keeps you ticking: your blood and all the nutrients you need. William Harvey, English court physician to King James I and King Charles I, discovered the circulatory system in the early 1600s. That's when he declared to the world his revolutionary and, at that time, controversial discovery: it is the blood circulating through the body that gives life.

Had the medical community paid closer attention to the Bible, they would have recognized this truth millennia sooner. In Leviticus 17:11, God told the Israelites, "The life of the flesh is in the blood." Not long ago, I talked with someone who had witnessed kidney-transplant surgery. This person said that when the transplant team brought in the donated kidney, it looked pale and anemic—like a piece of meat that had gone bad. But once they put the kidney in place and the patient's blood began to flow into it, the organ turned red, vibrant, and alive. The life of that kidney was in the blood that pulsed through it.

Of course, your blood would be of no help to you at all if your heart didn't do its job. That's why, as Simone and Roland discovered, taking care of your physical heart is literally a matter of life and death. Keep your heart free from disease, and it will keep you alive. Disregard the principles for heart health, and you run the risk of taking years off your life and bringing tragedy to your loved ones.

Heart specialists continue to perfect heart-transplant surgery. And perhaps someday there will be a technological breakthrough that will result in an efficient mechanical heart. But at this time, nothing can top the original equipment God designed for your body. Do everything you can to keep it working right.

*The two obvious keys to keeping your ticker ticking strongly are diet and exercise.* You just can't go through life on the run eating whatever is convenient and quick. If you want a healthy heart and a long life, you must be thoughtful and purposeful about your diet. We're not saying you have to give up juicy steaks and sugary desserts for life. That's no way to live either. You just have to be smart about what and how much you eat. In part 3, Drs. Duncan and Leachman will share with you a sensible, healthy, and realistic nutrition plan that includes foods you already enjoy.

As for exercise, you cannot assume that just because you live an active life, you get the exercise you really need for a healthy heart. Your physical workouts each week must be intentional, scheduled, and aimed at specific health goals. A good exercise plan will provide moderate exertion several times a week. And if you think all exercise is as boring as folding and ironing laundry, our physical heart health team has a pleasant surprise in store for you. Exercising your heart to better health can be fun!

## The Joy of a Healthy Spiritual Heart

Just as a healthy physical heart keeps your body well, so a healthy spiritual heart is essential to keeping the rest of you well. Wise King Solomon wrote, "Keep vigilant watch over your heart; *that's* where life starts" (Proverbs 4:23 MSG). The spiritual heart is mentioned more than eight hundred times in the

Bible. It's the spiritual heart we're talking about when we use words like *heartfelt*, *tender-hearted*, *hardhearted*, and *heartbreaking*. It's this heart we mean when we say, "My heart was touched," "My heart goes out to her," "God spoke to my heart," "She has a lot of heart," and "I'm sick at heart about it."

Flowing from the vital life center of the spiritual heart are our passions, our desires, our dreams, our characters, and our choices. Everyone can put on an act for a while. We can behave the way we know we should, say the right thing at the right time, and be the person others expect us to be. But eventually what's in our hearts is going to flow out. If the heart is not healthy, in time it will show up in our words, speech, decisions, responses, and reactions. That's why we must guard our hearts vigilantly. A healthy spiritual heart is essential to a healthy spiritual life.

The story I tell you now supposedly is true, though it defies our best efforts to document. In the early days of the United Nations, some of the most brilliant thinkers and scholars on the face of the earth gathered to draw up a plan for world peace. They wrote papers and delivered lecture after lecture. It sounded wonderful—the brotherhood of man, lasting peace in our time, paradise on earth as all nations and all cultures join in the common goal. Everyone was excited. It was unanimously agreed that this was going to work.

Then the presiding officer addressed the assembly and the gallery gathered to watch. "Are there any questions from anyone?"

A woman in the gallery raised her hand. "Yes," said the speaker.

She stood and said, "I'm a housewife here in New York, and I have three children. I'm so excited about world peace in our time. I'm so excited about what all these brilliant scholars have said. But I have one question."

"What is it, ma'am?" the officer said.

She replied, "What are you going to do about human nature?"

The scholars debated the question. Some of them got angry and began to argue. Before long, they were illustrating the very problem the insightful housewife had brought up. Whether this story is an urban legend or actually happened, it reminds us that peace of any kind—in the world, in a church, in a family—is a matter of human nature, which flows from the heart.

Unless you guard your heart, unless you pursue a healthy spiritual heart as well as a healthy physical heart, you will be vulnerable to life-crippling spiritual heart disease. How can you guard your heart? You let God go to work on it with His Word. There are at least three ways the Bible can keep your spiritual heart healthy.

## God's Word Makes Lifesaving Incisions Like a Scalpel

Hebrews 4:12–14 says, "His powerful Word is sharp as a surgeon's scalpel, cutting through everything, whether doubt or defense, laying us open to listen and obey. Nothing and no one is impervious to God's Word. We can't get away from it—no matter what" (MSG).

We all need spiritual heart surgery from time to time for strengthening weak muscles and cutting away diseased tissue. You need God's precise, healing Word in the hands of the Master Surgeon to keep your heart healthy and growing strong.

## God's Word Purifies and Cauterizes Like a Flame

The Lord spoke through the Old Testament prophet Jeremiah, "Is not My word like fire?" (Jeremiah 23:29). It's so easy to surround our hearts with rationalizations about what is right, what is good, and what we should do. Our human way of doing things tries to cut a deal with God based on our best ideas and plans. Isn't that the height of arrogance to try to tell God what to do? That's when we need the purifying, healing fire of the Word to burn away what is extraneous, that humanistic spin we tend to put on life.

## God's Word Crushes Like a Hammer

God is so lovingly concerned for the health of our hearts that He will sometimes resort to force. Still speaking through Jeremiah, the Lord continues, "Is not My word . . . like a hammer which shatters a rock?" (v. 29). Sometimes we are so hardhearted that God needs to allow difficult circumstances in our lives in order to turn our attention to His Word for solutions.

When a person needs open-heart surgery, the surgeon must inflict some damage and pain in order to get inside the rib cage and heal the heart. If he doesn't cut into the chest cavity, the disease can't be cured. His intent is not to be malicious or hurtful; he only wants to heal and nurture your heart to wholeness.

## Your Spiritual Heart Health Depends on You

The success of God's heart-healing work depends on an active response from you, just as maintaining a healthy physical heart requires you to be proactive with diet and exercise.

*You will encourage spiritual heart health by maintaining a consistent, personal connection with God.* Follow a daily plan that includes setting aside time to pray and read something from the Bible. We will talk more about going one-on-one with God later in this book.

*Staying healthy spiritually and physically is aided by being in church.* Many surveys have shown a positive link between church attendance and physical health. One study conducted by Robert Hummer of the University of Texas surveyed twenty-one thousand adults for a nine-year period. People who never attend church, the survey revealed, "are four times as likely to die from respiratory disease, diabetes, or infectious diseases."[1] When you are active in church, you are doing yourself and your health a huge favor!

What would you think about a heart-transplant patient who went back to the behavior that killed her first heart? As soon as she is dismissed from the hospital, she goes out and buys a case of cigarettes to continue a two-pack-a-day habit. She loads up on red meats and pastries at the market. She dines on fat-laden fast foods several times a week. She resumes a lifestyle of lounging around the house all day with no attempt at exercise. If you were her physician, you might want to take that new heart back and give it to someone who would take better care of it.

In most cases, however, there are few people as dedicated to proper diet and exercise as heart-disease survivors. Through the miracle of modern science and the skill of doctors like Mike Duncan and Rick Leachman, they have received a new lease on life. They know the value of keeping their hearts healthy. And they will do whatever is in their power to avoid damaging their hearts further.

Spiritual heart health is an ongoing discipline, just as physical heart health is. Interspersed between the insights on physical heart health from our two doctors, we will share helpful tips for keeping your spiritual heart strong and healthy by teaching you how to nurture it.

In the next chapter, our heart doctors will introduce you to the unique wonders of a woman's physical heart. It's one of the ways God made you special!

# Keys to Total Heart Health

## Chapter 2: The Wonder of a Woman's Heart

- The greatest natural wonder in God's created world is the human heart.

- God's design for your heart tells us something about His design for the rhythm of our lives: we need to rest and relax twice as long as we work.

- The two obvious keys to keeping your ticker ticking strongly are diet and exercise.

- Just as a healthy physical heart keeps your body well, so a healthy spiritual heart is essential for keeping the rest of you well.

- Flowing from the vital life center of the spiritual heart are our passions, our desires, our dreams, our characters, and our choices.

- To guard your heart, allow God to go to work on it with His Word, which makes lifesaving incisions like a surgeon's scalpel, purifies and cauterizes like a flame, and sometimes crushes like a hammer.

- The success of God's heart-healing work depends on an active response from you: you must maintain a consistent, personal connection with God; participate in church; and stay with the heart-healthy lifestyle.

- Spiritual heart health is an ongoing discipline, just as physical heart health is.

# 3
# What's So Special About Your Heart?

It pumps blood just like a man's but is affected by different hormones.

**Dr. Michael Duncan and Dr. Richard Leachman**

The story is told about a tough guy named Bruno who needed a heart transplant. At the time, there were only two hearts available: one donated by an old man who had died in poor health and another donated by a young woman in excellent health who had been killed in a car accident. Since the woman's heart was healthier, that's the one the surgeon put in during transplant surgery. But he decided not to tell Bruno that his new heart was from a woman, for obvious reasons.

A month after surgery, Bruno came into the clinic for a routine checkup. "How are you feeling, Bruno?" the doctor asked.

"Great, Doc," the patient replied. "The new heart is working fine."

"Have you experienced anything unusual since your surgery?" the doctor pressed.

"Well, Doc, there's one thing. Ever since I got my new heart, I've had this strong urge to wear something pink."

The doctor dismissed the comment with a wave of his hand. "It's no big deal, Bruno. A lot of guys today wear pink shirts or ties."

Bruno immediately burst into tears. "You're just like the guys down at the pool hall, Doc. You never listen to me, and you don't care about my feelings!"

Like most jokes, this one wanders a good distance from the truth to get a laugh. First, cardiovascular surgeons—or any other dedicated physicians for that matter—don't play games with their patients about diagnosis and treatment. Second, a human heart is not gender-specific; it doesn't come in different models for men and women. And third, a woman's physical heart is not the fountainhead of her emotions, hormones, and color preferences. All these exaggerations only serve to tickle the funny bone.

There is some truth in this story, however. For example, you may be interested to learn that a heart from a female donor can indeed be transplanted into a man, and vice versa. The two important criteria are blood type and body size. As long as blood type is compatible, the difference in body weight should be no greater than 15 percent, plus or minus. For example, a 160-pound woman or man can receive a heart from a donor of either sex weighing between 146 and 184 pounds. Obviously, if the heart is too small for the body, the demand on the heart will be too great. And if the heart is too large, it won't fit properly into the chest cavity.

Although a woman's heart is relatively interchangeable with a man's, there are some notable differences, particularly as they relate to the health of a woman's physical heart.

## Unique Characteristics Affecting a Woman's Heart

As Dr. and Mrs. Young mentioned, your heart is about the size of your fist. It weighs seven to fifteen ounces, depending on your overall body weight, and is roughly cone-shaped with the smaller end at the bottom. The human heart is made up of muscle tissue and is hollow so it can serve as a temporary reservoir for blood. The heart's function over your lifetime is to keep your blood circulating through the arteries, veins, and capillaries of your body. If you achieve normal life expectancy, your heart will beat about 3.5 billion times.

A woman's heart is generally smaller than a man's heart, simply because women on average are smaller than men in overall body size. Compare your fist with a man's fist to get an idea of the heart size difference. But there are other physical characteristics that set women apart from men. It is important for you to understand these differences, because they have an impact on your heart health.

## A Woman Has a Lower Metabolic Rate

Stacy and Mick carefully watch what they eat, and they run three miles a day together. But Mick is losing more weight than Stacy, which irritates her to no end. There's good reason for it, however. A woman's internal "engine" for processing calories runs at a slower speed than a man's, so it will take her longer to work off extra calories and pounds. Bottom line: the average woman must eat less and exercise more than the average man to achieve the same weight goals and overall health.

## A Woman's Cholesterol Is Different

Cholesterol is a significant concern in the pursuit of heart health because abnormal cholesterol levels in the blood are known to contribute to heart disease. There are two designations of cholesterol: high-density lipoprotein (HDL) and low-density lipoprotein (LDL). Most people know them as "good" cholesterol (HDL) and "bad" cholesterol (LDL). You may remember that high HDL scores are good and high LDL scores are bad.

As a woman, you enjoy a slight genetic benefit over a man when it comes to cholesterol. Women tend to have higher levels of good cholesterol and lower levels of bad cholesterol. This doesn't mean you can ignore the concerns about cholesterol in your diet. It just means you have a good head start in the right direction. After menopause, however, decreasing levels of estrogen in the system result in decreasing levels of HDL, meaning that a woman's cholesterol profile after menopause begins to look more like a man's. This change in profile also elevates the risk of heart problems in postmenopausal women.

## A Woman's Symptoms of Heart Attack and Other Heart Problems Are Different

Generally speaking, heart-attack symptoms in women are more diffuse and nonspecific than those in men. Typically, you hear of men complaining of chest pains and numbness in the left arm. While some women do experience these more typical symptoms, others experience pain at the top of the back, a burning sensation in the upper abdomen, nausea, flulike symptoms, anxiety, and sweating. Some women who suffer a heart attack don't even know it.

Furthermore, heart disease in women usually surfaces later in life than in men as a result of decreasing hormone levels. We have set apart chapter 6 for a thorough exploration of heart disease in women.

## A Woman's Hormones Impact Heart Health

The presence of estrogen in women up through midlife is thought to help protect against cardiovascular disease. But with the onset of menopause, women become more vulnerable to heart problems. Furthermore, since over-all health and vitality may be diminished due to aging after menopause, treating heart problems at this stage is more challenging.

## A Woman's Psychological Approach to Heart Health and Weight Loss Is Different

There are many factors that motivate persons to control their weight and pursue a healthy lifestyle. Women seem primarily motivated by benefits to their *appearance,* while men pursue these goals to increase their *strength.* While both qualities are desirable to both sexes, women tend to stay with diet and exercise to look good, while men do so to develop muscle.

# The Seasons of a Woman's Heart

God fashioned your physical heart to last for a long, long time. It has a life-time warranty! But like any product with a good warranty, there are conditions. As long as you follow the "manufacturer's guidelines," your heart will work hard to keep you healthy. Here's a look at a woman's heart through the decades and some important tips for keeping it strong.

## The Terrific Twenties

At age twenty-four, Jody was ready to conquer the world. Having just graduated from the university, she had a well-paying job, a new apartment two states removed from her parents' home, and big dreams for her life ahead. Jody was thrilled about being totally on her own now. She planned to live her own life without the shadow of Mom and Dad's rules hanging over her.

But it only took Jody a week to realize that she couldn't live without *some* rules. Showing up late for work two mornings, she drew a stern reprimand from her supervisor. So she bought a reliable clock radio and set the alarm for six o'clock. She also made sure to get her train fare on her way home each night so she wouldn't have to stop at the ATM in the morning. Jody knew if she didn't develop some good habits early, the independent life she had always dreamed about would be nothing more than that: a dream.

As Jody discovered, this first decade of adulthood is the time to set productive lifestyle patterns. The twenties is also the time to establish good heart health habits that will benefit you for the rest of your life. As a growing teenager, you could get by without paying close attention to what you ate. But when the growing years are over, maintaining normal weight for your height means eating healthful foods and getting sufficient exercise. Resist the temptation to plan your diet around convenience and cost. Learn to prepare meals that are nutritious and well balanced, keeping the total number of calories low. It can be done—even on a limited budget.

Join a gym, take aerobics classes at the local community center, or invest in a stairstepper, dumbbells, or an exercise machine. If you can't afford these exercise options, get into running, walking, or working out with one of dozens of video programs you can buy for pocket change at a garage sale. Start your life healthy, and you will likely stay healthy. *Your twenties is the best time in your life to launch into a Total Heart Health lifestyle!*

The most important decision you can make for your heart at this stage is to not smoke—or to stop smoking if you got into it as a teenager. Smoking is a heart killer.

The twenties may also launch you into marriage and childbearing. If so, give special attention to proper nutrition, including vitamin supplementation for you and your baby. And please note: *folate, or folic acid, is vitally important during the childbearing years for you and the baby inside you.* Consult your physician to make sure you are getting sufficient quantities of folate in your diet. In chapters 13 and 14, we will explore more fully the diet and dietary supplements important to women at all life stages.

## The Thrilling Thirties

Childbearing can take a toll on a woman's figure, and a busy life of career and/or homemaking and parenting can seriously challenge her commitment to a regimen of diet and exercise. As one thirty-something woman groused, "I've got a husband, three young children—two of them still in diapers—and a part-time job. And I'm supposed to exercise thirty minutes a day? Get serious!"

Yes, the career and/or family demands at this stage can be taxing. It will take some creative planning to maintain a Total Heart Health lifestyle through the thirties. If you're a mother, keep your eyes open for a gym, club, or community center that offers childcare for a nominal charge during exercise classes. Arrange a childcare swap with a friend, relative, or neighbor, allowing you to work out at home or at a club. And it is important to maintain healthy eating habits for you and your family. Your kids may not believe it at first, but prove to them that healthy meals served at the family dinner table can actually taste good! In the process, use this time to teach them about good nutrition.

Often during this decade, hypertension (high blood pressure) and lipid (cholesterol) abnormalities begin to manifest themselves. It's important to schedule regular checkups with your physician so any problems can be diagnosed early and treated.

## The Fabulous Forties

As a single career woman, Abby took full advantage of one of the great perks her company offered: health-club membership. She worked out at the club for thirty to forty minutes several times a week. But another "work perk" backfired on her. She was responsible for entertaining clients at breakfast or lunch, so she was eating out on the company nickel three or four days a week. Even though she enjoyed the food and loved making clients happy, she began to put on a few pounds—despite her workout routine. Abby realized she had to be more careful when she scanned the menu. When she was, her exercise program helped her get back to her target weight.

Women in their forties are fully involved in career pursuits, family activities, or both. This is the decade when some women begin to put on weight. Increased earnings and a higher standard of living often accompany career success at this stage. And with more discretionary income comes the temptation to eat richer foods and dine out more often, resulting in greater calorie intake. Some women eat more at this stage in response to stress and life pressures.

Also, as energy begins to wane, forty-something women may become lax when it comes to exercise, resulting in fewer calories burned. More calories taken in coupled with fewer calories worked out equals weight gain. Disciplined diet and exercise are a must at this stage to avoid unwanted pounds.

For many women, menopause begins in the mid- to late forties. During menopause, the ovaries, which have produced eggs for four decades or more, begin to shut down production. And since the developing eggs supply estrogen, that supply decreases as menopause approaches and then ceases altogether. Important note: any signs of high blood pressure or cholesterol problems must be treated aggressively with medication. This is also the time for your doctor to check for the presence of latent diabetes, especially if you are overweight.

## The Fantastic Fifties

This is the decade when many women ride an emotional and hormonal roller coaster. For those who married and started families in their twenties, the kids are grown and leaving home for college, marriage, and career. Those who delayed parenting until midlife may still have children at home, but the empty nest is within sight. Let's be honest here: as much as we want our children to move into adulthood, it's not easy—and sometimes it's downright tough—to see our chicks leave the nest.

Even though it may be a time of sadness, the season of the empty nest is also a time for taking on tasks you have put off through the busy child-rearing years. It's a time when many wives and husbands rediscover the romance and fun that sometimes get buried under an avalanche of carpooling, kids' sports and school programs, and career building. It's a time to get serious about the plans, dreams, vacations, and hobbies you just didn't have time for while the kids were still at home. And with education expenses reduced, now's the time to get that fitness-club membership you've always wanted.

Concurrent with the empty nest experience, menopause concludes. The disappearance of estrogen allows good cholesterol (HDL) to decrease and bad cholesterol (LDL) to increase. So if you are in your fifties, *it is very important to closely monitor your cholesterol and blood pressure and keep your weight in check.*

## The Sensational Sixties—and Beyond

Sometimes when little Megan says "Grandma," Jaye looks around for an old lady in the room. Jaye can't believe that at the young age of sixty-two, she has a granddaughter in preschool. And when she went in for her annual checkup, Jaye experienced another shock. Her blood pressure was dangerously high. "I've never had a problem with high blood pressure before!" she exclaimed to her doctor.

It is during their sixties when most women see the first clear manifestation of cardiovascular disease (CVD). Therefore, *any noticeable change in health, such as the sudden onset of fatigue or flulike symptoms, should be taken seriously, and medical treatment should be sought right away.* As always, proper nutrition, along with vitamin supplementation and medication for hypertension and cholesterol abnormalities, should be faithfully continued during this stage.

It is also important at this stage of life to keep exercising. You probably won't be able to crank the treadmill up to top speed like you did when you were thirty or forty, but the good news is you don't need to. Just maintain an active life as much as possible and spend at least thirty minutes a day in some form of regimented exercise: walking or jogging (on the treadmill, in the neighborhood, or in the local indoor mall), playing a sport such as tennis or paddleball, or working out on a resistance machine set to accommodate your level of strength.

A lot has been written and discussed recently about hormone replacement therapy (HRT). At first HRT was widely recommended by doctors for most women past "the change" to relieve postmenopausal symptoms, such as hot flashes and bone loss, and to aid in the prevention of cardiovascular disease. However, *the most recent American Heart Association guidelines do not recommend hormone replacement therapy for primary or secondary prevention of heart disease or for use in women with known heart disease.* Studies do not show a significant benefit in heart disease prevention, and the use of HRT raises the possibility of a short-term increase in risk.

Most cardiologists agree that hormones may be considered for non-heart benefits, including symptomatic relief of menopause.[1] However, *because the complications of HRT use increase the longer it is used, HRT should be used only for the shortest time necessary.* Women should weigh the risks of HRT and discuss them with their doctor.

No matter what decade you find yourself in, physical heart health is both important and achievable. Don't allow the duties and demands of these normal life stages to rob your heart of the care it deserves. Whether you're a single twenty-something or a grandmother, now is the time to establish a healthy heart lifestyle. We encourage you to begin your journey with the 90-Day Challenge summarized in chapter 20.

A woman's spiritual heart is as unique and special as her physical heart. Dr. and Mrs. Young will now tell you why.

# Keys to Total Heart Health

## Chapter 3: What's So Special About Your Heart?

- Although a woman's heart is relatively interchangeable with a man's, there are some notable differences, particularly as they relate to the health of a woman's physical heart.

- A woman's heart is generally smaller than a man's.

- A woman has a lower metabolic rate.

- A woman's cholesterol is different.

- A woman's symptoms of heart attack and other heart problems are different.

- A woman's hormones before and after menopause impact heart health.

- A woman's psychological approach to heart health and weight loss is different.

- In their twenties, women begin to set productive lifestyle patterns.

- In their thirties, women may discover high blood pressure and cholesterol problems.

- In their forties, some women begin to put on weight, as they eat more to deal with stress and exercise less.

- In their fifties, women who have gone through menopause should monitor their cholesterol and blood pressure and keep their weight in check.

- In their sixties and beyond, most women see the first clear manifestation of cardiovascular disease and should see a doctor regularly.

# 4
# Your Heart Connection with God

You have the same spiritual capacity as a man but a different concept of God.

**Ed and Jo Beth Young**

Edwin and I learned about a couple in our city who adopted two young girls from China. The face of one of the little girls was marred by a deformity, so when the adopting parents brought her back to Houston, they arranged for corrective surgery. When the bandages finally came off, the girl's face was greatly improved, but it wasn't perfect. Her natural beauty had been scarred for life. Yet this loving mother exclaimed with joy, "Just look at her; she's perfect!" I was amazed at how this mom viewed her new daughter and was moved by the depth of her unconditional love.

This story reminds me that there are two ways you can look at your spiritual heart. You may look at what's inside and think it's not very pretty. You're all too aware of the places where you are hard and unyielding toward God and soft and compromising toward self and worldly attractions. Your heart may seem quick to break and slow to heal. You may wish your emotions weren't always so close to the surface. You feel prone to flareups of anger and icy indifference—even toward God. All this complicates the way you relate to God, and you wonder how He could love you.

Or you can look at your heart the way this loving mother viewed her scarred child, which reflects how God looks at you. You can accept yourself the way you are, even though you're not perfect. You can relate to God just as you are—emotions and all—because it's the way God made you. Sure, you have room to grow and mature in your relationship with God. But if you have placed your faith in Christ, God sees you as perfect in His Son and accepts you unconditionally. You need to see yourself the same way.

## Cherishing Your Unique Beauty

God created women to be different from men, and He did it on purpose. Sexuality is no accident, no evolutionary tweak that assures the perpetuation of the race. You are a woman by God's design, and He likes you the way you are as a female.

After each stage of creation recorded in the book of Genesis, God viewed what He made and said, "It is good." The Hebrew word for "good" suggests cheer and pleasure. God sighed with happiness over the result of His creative work. But it wasn't until He formed man and then woman that God announced, "It is *very* good" (see Genesis 1:31). Only after Eve was in the garden did God use a superlative!

### Physically Different

Physically, the differences between men and women are notable. Take the way we typically relate to heat and cold, for instance. We heard about a woman who said that the thermostat is the number one marriage-breaker in America. She contends that every engaged couple should be locked in a room for eight straight hours with a thermostat as an indication of how their marriage will survive their differences.

Edwin and I have radically different views of the thermostat. He's hot natured, and I shiver even in the tropics. After dating me for six years, Edwin knew exactly what to give me for Christmas. I opened my gift to find an electric blanket with dual controls. That's also when my parents figured out that things were getting serious between us.

After we were married, one night the dual controls got mixed up. Shortly after switching on the blanket, Edwin was melting, so he twirled the dial he thought was his down to low. As he did, I began to turn to a block of ice, so I twisted the dial on my side up to high. Without knowing it, I was broiling Edwin to "well done" while he was flash-freezing me!

That's right, women are physically different from men in many ways, and we are free to fully enjoy this difference.

## Emotionally Different

Men and women are wired differently emotionally, and research has shown that our wiring has everything to do with how we respond to situations. For example, when little boys come up against obstacles, they tend to push them out of the way while girls tend to go around them. Who taught boys and girls to handle obstacles differently? Nobody. It's just the way God made them. Studies have shown that when a six-month-old girl hears jazz music playing, her heart-beat increases. But when a six-month-old boy hears jazz, he shows absolutely no physical response at all. How did they learn these different responses at such a tender age? They didn't learn the responses; it's the way God wired them.

Some experts suggest that men equate maturity with independence, while women view maturity in terms of interdependence. You may have noticed this difference in your relationships with a husband, father, brother, or grown son. Men are out to make their mark in the world, whether it be in a career, a mission, or a hobby. These pursuits often take them away from relationships for great periods of time. But women are driven more by togetherness in relationships, both with girlfriends and with husband or male friends.

The way you are is the product of an inner mechanism, the makeup of your soul, your emotions, your very heart. Independence and interdependence are both God-given qualities. Men are generally more gifted at independence; women are more gifted at interdependence. Neither is wrong, though they can be expressed in wrong ways.

## Spiritually Different

Women are also wired differently in how they relate to God. If you don't believe it, consider how a women's retreat differs from a men's retreat.

Laura is a member of the women's ministry staff at our church. For a retreat theme, Laura says she would go with an issue drawn from current events but shaped for a spiritual retreat. "Extreme Makeover" is an idea Laura likes. She would invite speakers and arrange breakout sessions on makeover topics like cosmetics and hairstyles while challenging women to welcome the makeover of spirit, mind, and emotions. The program would carve out time for women to sit together in small groups with coffee and talk about their problems and needs.

Laura would select a comfortable retreat center not far from a mall or town so ladies could enjoy shopping during free time. Great attention and expense would be focused on motif, including platform appearance, table decorations, centerpieces, and even gift baskets waiting in the guests' rooms. The menu would feature healthy gourmet meals. Laura would also arrange for after-school childcare so moms could leave for the retreat on Friday afternoon.

Roger is a pastor and a real man's man. He once played professional golf and hosted a TV show on hunting and fishing. His idea of a retreat for men would be utterly different.

Roger would focus a men's retreat on themes like integrity, loyalty, and leadership qualities. His guest speakers would be drawn from the ranks of coaches, military leaders, business leaders, and political activists. The retreat site would be somewhere in the country, the more rustic the better, and the menu would center on mass quantities of anything that can be served with cream gravy. Decorations would take a backseat to a high-powered sound system, a PowerPoint setup, and a monstrous TV for watching football on Saturday afternoon. Other free-time activities would include target shooting, basketball, a golf tournament, and fishing.

I'll bet you can't wait to go to one of Roger's retreats! No? Well, the men you know probably feel the same way about the retreats you attend.

When it comes to a woman's spiritual heart, I (Edwin) see at least three ways in which God wired you differently from a man.

*Women tend to trust God and surrender to His authority.* This is not to say that women lack the capacity for strong leadership. The large number of female leaders in business and government throughout the world attests to this quality. But even with strong leadership traits, women bring to their relationships with God an ability to open their hearts to His authority. What has mistakenly been termed gullibility in women is really the wonderful quality of "trustability."

When Jo Beth and I fell in love, we didn't know we would spend our lives in Christian ministry. One day I came home and said, "I feel that God wants me to become a preacher, and I don't understand it." But Jo Beth didn't have a problem with it. She embraced the idea wholeheartedly. At one point, we had to move from a beautiful rural location to a noisy, crowded urban setting. The move made no sense to me, and I hesitated to tell Jo Beth about it. But when I did, Jo Beth simply said, "If God wants us to go, let's go."

Jo Beth has always been more ready to trust God's leading than I have. Had it not been for my wife's capacity to trust God—and to trust her husband when he heard God speak—we might have missed what God has done through us over the years.

God has equipped women with a tenderness and pliability with regard to His authority. This is a wonderful gift that will equip you for accomplishing great things in all the paths where God is leading you.

*Women are more process-driven; men are more goal-driven.* Men tend to focus on getting something done: closing the sale, fixing the problem, earning the promotion. Women tend to focus on *how* things get done. This may be the reason some women are chosen for leadership in business.

Being process-driven, women are more attuned to prayer as a vital element in the process of spiritual transformation. Men, who are generally goal-driven, see spiritual growth as a series of steps to be mastered: read the book, attend the seminar, complete the study project. While women also gain much from these steps, they are more focused on processing input than checking off a list of spiritual accomplishments. And being more relational than men, women see prayer as the opportunity to process in relationship with God.

Women tend to work out their problems and challenges through their earthly relationships. That's why you probably log more hours on the phone talking with relatives and friends than a man does. Guys want to fix the problem; girls need to talk it through. Guys tend to "go it alone"; girls seek and welcome others who will commiserate with them and counsel them.

*Women are more readily dependent on God's leadership.* In some ways, women are stronger than men, such as in the generally accepted ability to endure pain better than men. But women also have an innate aversion to exposure and aloneness, which translates into the positive quality of welcoming the support, protection, and leadership of others. As such, women are blessed with greater responsiveness to God's leadership than most men and a greater tendency to yield to His direction than to challenge it.

The great classic love stories tell some version of a brave champion who rescues a woman in distress. Women want their dads, their big brothers, and their husbands to be champions who will protect them from danger. Obviously, God is the ultimate champion, rescuer, and provider, so women are generally more ready to seek and accept His leadership and provision, while men tend to find their own way before yielding to God's authority.

Welcoming God as leader, some women feel that they don't measure up to what He expects of them and can't keep up with His leadership. He's their leader, but He seems to be way out front. But it's this sense of inadequacy that opens the door to another positive feminine quality: a strong sense of God's grace. Women seem to understand better than men that rule keeping and accomplishment cannot make up for human inadequacy. It takes grace, big batches of it.

This grace sense is reflected in a woman's role as grace-giver in relationships. God seems to have better equipped men for leadership and better equipped women for closeness. When a toddler falls and scrapes a knee, most of the time she will head for Mom for comfort and a warm embrace. Even when caught in a wrong, kids tend to prefer their moms, whom they view as more understanding and patient. Moms inherit this ability to comfort and console from their view of God, who leads them with grace and forgiveness.

Women are wonderfully equipped in many marvelous ways. But just because God has designed you this way doesn't mean you can coast through life on your traits. You need to take care to nurture a strong spiritual heart.

## Enhancing Your Unique Beauty

Here are four positive qualities that mark a strong spiritual heart. I (Jo Beth) call them "The Four Gs." As you seek to strengthen these qualities in your life, you will fortify your inner heart to withstand anything life throws at you.

## A Grateful Heart

I remember how my heart was thrilled when each of our grandchildren learned to express their gratitude. Their simple "T'ank oo" in kid's vernacular couldn't have been more eloquent. Our words of thanks also bring delight to God's heart. Thankfulness is one of the most obvious revelations of God's will in Scripture. Paul says it plainly: "Thank God no matter what happens" (1 Thessalonians 5:18 MSG). It gives God pleasure when we acknowledge Him with gratitude.

The real test of a grateful heart is when you don't *feel* very thankful for what's happening. Learn to say, "Thank You, Lord," even when a friend stands you up for lunch, a child spills his milk all over your dinner plate, your boss criticizes you unfairly, the dog tracks mud into the house, and so on. The Bible doesn't say, "*Feel* thankful"; it says, "*Give* thanks." Practicing thankfulness in the small trials of life will prepare your heart for responding positively to life's big challenges and tragedies.

## A Growing Heart

The physical heart stops growing in size when we reach adulthood. If it didn't stop growing, you would be in trouble. In fact, if you are diagnosed with an enlarged heart, you need to be under the care of a heart specialist. But our spiritual hearts have tremendous capacity for growth. There is always room for developing greater love for our family and friends, more compassion for people in need, and deeper devotion to God. There is no point at which we can say our spiritual hearts have arrived. A healthy spiritual heart keeps growing. We will talk more about some of the aspects of a growing heart in the chapters ahead.

## A Giving Heart

Most women are gracious givers by nature, but the art of giving still needs to be cultivated over a lifetime. Families can be demanding on us in many ways. Friends are sometimes sponges for our time and attention. Employers want to squeeze their money's worth and more out of us. Nowhere does the Bible say we are to be doormats to the whims of everyone else. But Jesus encouraged us, "Live generously" (Matthew 10:8 MSG). A giving heart is a healthy heart.

## A Grounded Heart

Someone once gave me a live plant in a thin plastic pot. I took the plant out to the backyard and placed it, plastic pot and all, on the soil in a large clay pot on the ground. It stayed there for a couple of years. When the clay pot got inadvertently knocked over, my plant went with it. But when I tried to pick it up, I couldn't lift it. I discovered that its roots had grown through the bottom of the plastic pot, down through the bottom of the clay pot, and into the ground. I couldn't move it without cutting away some of its roots.

This is a beautiful picture of a grounded heart. A healthy spiritual heart must be deeply rooted in God's Word. The Bible must be an integral part of your daily life. Read it, memorize it, quote it, listen to it, sing it, meditate on it, talk about it with your friends, and teach it to your children. As you pour the Word into your life, it will serve as an anchor against the forces opposing a healthy heart.

That's right: there are forces arrayed against your physical and spiritual heart. In the next part of the book, we will unmask them and show you how to nullify their harmful attacks.

# Keys to Total Heart Health

## Chapter 4: Your Heart Connection with God

- There are two ways you can look at your spiritual heart. One is to look at what's inside and think it's not very pretty. The other way is to accept yourself even though you're not perfect and realize you can relate to God just as you are.

- Sexuality is no accident. You are a woman by God's design, and He likes you the way you are as a female.

- When it comes to a woman's spiritual heart, there are at least three ways God wired women differently from men:

  1. Women tend to trust God and surrender to His authority.

  2. Women are more process-driven; men are more goal-driven.

  3. Women are more dependent on God's leadership.

- Four positive qualities mark a strong spiritual heart: a grateful heart, a growing heart, a giving heart, and a grounded heart.

- The Bible must be an integral part of your daily life. As you pour the Word into your life, it will serve as an anchor against the forces opposing a healthy heart.

# Part Two

The Enemies
of a Woman's Heart

# 5
# Your Heart Is a Target

God wants you to enjoy a rich, full life;
but someone else has other plans.

**Ed and Jo Beth Young**

Someone very powerful and devious is dead set against the healthy heart God wants you to have. This enemy's target is the heart of every woman and man, and he is particularly interested in ruining the lives of people who want to take God seriously. This enemy, of course, is the enemy of our souls and God's archenemy: Satan himself.

Now, please don't think Jo Beth and I are going off the deep end spiritually and insisting that there is a demon under every rock and behind every door just waiting to grab us and carry us away against our will. Nor are we saying that the devil is personally responsible for everything wrong and hurtful in our lives. We are imperfect people living in an imperfect world, and hurtful things happen. But if you dismiss the sobering biblical reality that Satan is out to keep you from God's goodness in your life, you will be especially vulnerable to his destructive schemes, and your total heart will be at great risk.

The conflict between what God has for us and what Satan intends to do about it is no more clearly and concisely stated than in John 10:10. Jesus said, "A thief is only there to steal and kill and destroy. I came so they can have real and eternal life, more and better life than they ever dreamed of" (MSG). We really like the second half of that verse, don't we, especially the idea of a better, more abundant life? It is often quoted all by itself, as if the first half of the verse didn't exist. But watch out: there really is a thief plotting against you.

The abundant life that Jesus describes here is even better than most of us have imagined. Two Greek words in the New Testament are translated "life."

One of them is *bios*, referring to biological life, natural life. We can't live in a world of time, space, and matter without biological structure—a living body, breathing, eating, and conforming to natural laws. The other word translated "life," which occurs in John 10:10, is *zoe*, meaning spiritual life, life on God's plane. When you see the phrase "everlasting life" or "eternal life" in the New Testament, the word translated "life" is *zoe*. It's the same word Jesus used when announcing, "I am the way, and the truth, and the life" (John 14:6); "I am the bread of life" (John 6:35); and "I am the resurrection and the life" (John 11:25).

We received *bios* when we were conceived and born into this world. Jesus came to bring us *zoe*, which not only infinitely enhances the quality of our biological existence but supersedes it both now and throughout eternity. And in John 10:10, Jesus qualified the life He gives with the word *abundantly*, meaning "over and above; more than necessary." It's the same picture Paul used to describe our God, who can do anything, "far more than you could ever imagine or guess or request in your wildest dreams!" (Ephesians 3:20 MSG).

Why has God lavished the fullness of His life on us? It's not just for our benefit. It goes far beyond our mere fulfillment and enjoyment. As Rick Warren so beautifully reminds us in *The Purpose Driven Life*, "You were made *by* God and *for* God—and until you understand that, life will never make sense. . . . Life is about letting God use you for *his* purposes."[1] We have God's abundant life *in us* so God's abundant love can flow *through us* to touch the hearts of other people.

## Your Heart's Number One Enemy

God's glorious purposes for your life are precisely why Satan is your sworn enemy. He is diametrically opposed to everything God is and does; so if you're in God's camp, you are Satan's target. But he's not out just to wound you; he's aiming for your heart. He wants to neutralize your impact for Christ in the world. He wants to kill your heart.

How does he do it? John 10:10 uses three words: *steal, kill,* and *destroy.* "Steal" in this verse is the Greek word *klepto*, from which we get our English word *kleptomaniac*—an impulsive thief. The word *thief* in this verse comes from the same root. It means to sneak in and take something by stealth. The devil is out to filch every good thing God has given to you. It's the same picture we get in the parable of the soils when Jesus said, "The devil comes and takes away *[klepto]* the word from their heart, so that they will not believe and be saved" (Luke 8:12).

But Satan doesn't burst in to rob you with guns blazing. He's a con artist, a scammer. We are to be wary of his "schemes" (Ephesians 6:11), which are cunning, deceitful, and crafty. He wants to fool with your mind and trick you out of the good things God has given you before you know what hit you.

"Kill" has no secret, obscure meaning; it means to put to death, like an animal slaughtered for a sacrifice. In Romans 12:1, Paul urges us to present ourselves to God as living sacrifices. By stark contrast, Satan just wants us dead. He will do everything in his power to snuff out our spiritual life. He can't take away our salvation, but he can do his best to separate us from life-sustaining involvement in God's Word, in prayer, and in fellowship with other Christians.

Satan not only wants to suffocate your spiritual heart; he will do whatever he can to take away your physical heart. Jesus labeled the devil a "murderer" (John 8:44). Satan is out to cause your physical death if he possibly can. Why does Satan want you physically dead? Because it would bring an abrupt end to your loving care for others, the purpose to which God has called you. With you out of the way, he has eliminated a key person God wants to use to touch your family members, your neighbors, your friends, and others in your circle of influence.

How can he get rid of you? Well, he knows you're too smart to fall for the temptation to jump off a bridge, throw yourself in front of a speeding train, or drink a bottle of cyanide—although he may introduce such drastic thoughts when you're discouraged or depressed. Remember: he's a con artist. He wants to trick you into doing his bidding, to cause you to think it's not so bad. So he might just suggest more acceptable behaviors that could eventually gain him the same result, behaviors that will negatively affect your health.

We cannot presume that we are physically invincible just because we are Christians. If we mistreat our bodies through poor diet and lack of proper exercise, we will pay the price for it. Such irresponsible behavior may not kill us outright, but it may open the door to such problems as heart disease or cancer, which will usher death into the picture before its time. And in the meantime, the enemy can disrupt and disable our lives through sickness, which also thwarts God's purposes for us in the world.

Jesus also said the devil comes to "destroy," which means to render useless. He is always intent on destroying our abundance and vitality, leaving our lives a barren desert and useless ruin. Ethel Waters, the late, great old-time gospel singer, used to say, "God don't make no junk." But the devil specializes in filling our lives with junk. He can't make you into junk, but he can tempt you to believe you are no good to God or anybody. In this way he will try to destroy you physically, emotionally, spiritually, intellectually, and relationally.

How does the enemy go about his business of stealing, killing, and destroying? The New Testament reveals many of Satan's strategies designed to trick you into thoughts and deeds that will ruin your heart and render you useless to God and others. Here are some of them:

- He tempts us to do the opposite of what God wants (see 1 Thessalonians 3:5).

- He works to oppress us, meaning to exercise harsh control (see Acts 10:38).

- He seeks to devour us, swallow us (see 1 Peter 5:8).

- He tries to bind us, tie us up, and keep us from moving forward (see Luke 13:16).

- He disguises himself to look attractive and appealing (see 2 Corinthians 11:14).

- He hinders us, meaning to block our course or cut us off (see 1 Thessalonians 2:18).

- He lies to us, because he is a liar by nature (see John 8:44).

## The Enemy's "Accomplices"

As mentioned earlier, we don't believe the Bible teaches that the devil or even one of his demons is personally responsible for every lapse you suffer in the care of your physical and spiritual heart. He is certainly at the root of all the evil we suffer, but he has some "accomplices" that do much of his dirty work for him.

## Lust

One of Satan's accomplices is lust, which is the longing or desire to please our flesh and to get what we want as opposed to pleasing and obeying God. James wrote, "The temptation to give in to evil comes from us and only us. We have no one to blame but the leering, seducing flare-up of our own lust. Lust gets pregnant, and has a baby: sin! Sin grows up to adulthood, and becomes a real killer" (James 1:14–15 MSG).

Lust arises from the old habits, feelings, and thoughts we lived by before God made our hearts come alive through Christ. These old selfish patterns keep demanding their own way. When we obey these lustful longings, we sin; and those sins move us in the direction of disease and death to the total heart.

## The Godless World System

Another one of Satan's accomplices in attacking our hearts is the godless world system in which we live. The apostle John wrote, "Practically everything that goes on in the world—wanting your own way, wanting everything for yourself, wanting to appear important—has nothing to do with the Father. It just isolates you from him" (1 John 2:16 MSG). Much of our lust is triggered by what we see, hear, and experience in a world that puts selfish pleasures above God.

For example, as you well know, the world bombards us with images of immorality through the media: movies, television, novels, and magazines. Faithful monogamy and sex reserved only for marriage are portrayed as archaic and odd, while adultery, illicit affairs, and casual sex between consenting adults and teens are glorified as normal and right. Being exposed to so many episodes of bedroom roulette in the media—and in the public lives of our favorite celebrities—we may wonder if God's view of moral purity is outdated. No wonder so many Christians today, including some of our respected leaders, are caving in to sexual temptation.

The world's misguided idea of right and wrong comes at us from every direction, tempting us to compromise biblical standards for honesty, truth, righteousness, humility, service to others, and so on. Falling prey to this accomplice of the enemy will weaken your heart instead of strengthening it.

And look at how the world attacks your physical heart. So many advertisements on TV make unhealthy foods look desirable and convenient. Why cook good food at home when it's so easy and inexpensive to drive through a fast-food place—any time of the day or night? Why order a regular-sized portion of French fries when the large and extra-large portions cost only a little more? The food industry is out to make money, so their ads will promote quantity, convenience, and flavor over sensible portions and healthy ingredients.

If we allow the world to sway us with its message about food, the fallout will diminish the health of our physical hearts. Drs. Duncan and Leachman will talk more specifically about these dangers in the chapters ahead.

## Be On Guard for Your Heart's Sake

Solomon had keen insight into the assault of the world, the flesh, and the devil on the total heart, leaving us the important directive "Guard your heart" (Proverbs 4:23 NLT). His wise warning must be heeded. The abundant life Christ has for us is under constant attack. If you don't fight for the health of your total heart, who will?

How can you stand up to the enemy's malicious opposition? The Word of God provides some straightforward, hope-filled answers.

### Keep Alert to the Enemy's Attempts to Attack You

God's Word warns us, "Keep a cool head. Stay alert. The Devil is poised to pounce, and would like nothing better than to catch you napping. Keep your guard up" (1 Peter 5:8 MSG). Don't minimize Satan's cunning, which is more dangerous than a stalking, hungry lion out for a kill.

### Send the Enemy Packing

Peter says about the roaring lion, "Resist him, firm in your faith" (1 Peter 5:9). James says, "So let God work his will in you. Yell a loud *no* to the Devil and watch him scamper" (James 4:7 MSG). For all his craft and cunning, Satan is outranked by a believer who is submitted to the authority of Christ, and he must obey your orders. Whenever this conniving thief and liar or one of his accomplices threatens your heart, you have every right in Christ to tell him to get lost.

In God's unsearchable wisdom, He has called you and equipped you for this battle for your heart. *You* must be alert. *You* must resist the enemy of your heart in Christ's power and authority. As you do, you are being effectively proactive in improving your Total Heart Health.

Before we look closer at some other ways your spiritual heart is under attack, Drs. Duncan and Leachman will alert us to some serious threats to your physical heart. Guarding your physical heart is an important element in our 90-Day Challenge and Total Heart Health lifestyle.

# Keys to Total Heart Health
## Chapter 5: Your Heart Is a Target

- The enemy of our souls is dead set against the healthy heart God desires for us, and the heart is Satan's target.

- Jesus came to bring us *zoe* (spiritual life), which not only infinitely enhances the quality of our biological existence but supersedes it both now and throughout eternity.

- We have God's abundant life *in us* so that God's abundant love can flow *through us* to touch the hearts of other people.

- God has a purpose for your life, and that's why Satan is your enemy. Satan wants to neutralize your impact for Christ in the world.

- Satan doesn't burst in to rob you with guns blazing. He's a con artist, a scammer. He wants to trick you into doing his bidding, to cause you to think it's not so bad.

- If we mistreat our bodies through poor diet and lack of proper exercise, we will open the door to heart disease or cancer, which will usher death into the picture before its time.

- The devil is at the root of all evil we suffer, and he has some "accomplices": lust, the godless world system, fallen culture, moral relativism, and alluring temptations.

- To stand up to the enemy's malicious opposition, the Bible tells us to stay alert to the enemy's attempts to attack us, and to send the enemy packing.

# 6
# Heart Health—
# A Real Life-and-Death Matter

If you're not heart savvy,
"love handles" are just the tip of the iceberg.

**Dr. Michael Duncan and Dr. Richard Leachman**


Ruth will never forget the night she almost lost her husband. Bernie was jogging on the treadmill in the basement when Ruth, who was sorting laundry nearby, heard him gasp and moan. "Don't worry, dear," Bernie said, grimacing and doubled over. "It's just a gas pain under my heart." Then he rubbed his left arm and hissed in pain.

"It might be worse than you think," Ruth said, alarmed. "Chest pain and left arm pain: those are symptoms of a heart attack. I'm taking you to the emergency room."

Bernie resisted, but Ruth would not be denied. Within thirty minutes they were at the hospital. At six the next morning, Bernie was wheeled into surgery for quadruple-bypass surgery.

That was three years ago, and Bernie has been grateful ever since that Ruth dragged him to the emergency room that night. So when Ruth thought she had a serious case of the flu, which left her feeling like she had been hit by a train, it was Bernie who insisted, "We need to get you to the doctor."

Ruth put up a weak argument, saying she would be fine in a few days. But Bernie would have nothing of it. Arriving at the hospital, they had to sit in the ER waiting room for more than an hour while patients with more serious problems were attended to. After all, it was only the flu.

But it wasn't the flu, and Ruth was admitted to the hospital for angioplasty to remove a potentially lethal coronary artery blockage. "But I didn't have pain in my chest or my left arm," Ruth said, bewildered.

"That's probably because you're a woman," the cardiologist explained. "Cardiovascular disease is almost as prevalent in women as it is in men, but the symptoms can be quite different. It's just a good thing your husband brought you here in time. Your undiagnosed and untreated 'flu' might have killed you."

## The Number One Heart Killer

Cardiovascular disease (CVD) is the number one health threat to women and the leading cause of death in the United States and the Western world. *Cardiovascular disease* is a generic term inclusive of a number of maladies afflicting the heart and coronary arteries, such as atherosclerosis (plaque buildup in the arteries), stroke, and heart attack. The American Heart Association reports that CVD claims more women's lives than the next seven causes of death combined—nearly five hundred thousand women a year.[1]

Despite heart disease being the most common cause of death in women, most women are unaware of the seriousness of the problem. By and large they accept that cancer is the most likely cause of death, and in particular they fear breast cancer.[2] The threat of breast cancer is getting a lot of media coverage these days. You've seen the little pink ribbons signifying breast cancer awareness; perhaps you wear one yourself. And you probably know about national and regional campaigns organized to find a cure for breast cancer. To be sure, breast cancer is a killer: one in every twenty-five women will die of breast cancer. Yet the mortality rate from breast cancer pales in comparison to that of cardiovascular disease. Half of all women will die of CVD, including heart attack, stroke, peripheral vascular disease (poor circulation to the feet or legs), or heart failure—*one out of every two women!* CVD is the "silent killer" among women because it doesn't get the media attention of cancer, especially breast cancer.[3]

Overall, the prevalence of heart disease in men is slightly higher than in women, but heart disease increases proportionately in women in every age group up into the sixties. In the sixty-five to seventy-four age group, women finally catch up to men, with an equal prevalence of CVD in both sexes. Above age seventy-five, women surpass men in the prevalence of heart disease.[4] Statistically, as a woman, the older you get, the greater your risk of some form of cardiovascular disease.[5]

What is even more disconcerting is that the incidence of CVD-related deaths is *decreasing* in men but *increasing* in women. Here's what the studies reveal:

- During the last twenty-five years, the number of deaths attributed to cardiovascular disease in men has declined from 510,000 to less than 440,000. During the same time frame, female deaths have increased from 490,000 to nearly 510,000.[6]

- Women are more likely than men to die after a cardiac event. Thirty-eight percent of women who have had a heart attack die within one year; only 25 percent of men die within one year.[7]

- Sixty-three percent of women who die suddenly have no prior diagnosis of cardiovascular disease, compared to 50 percent of men.

- Within six years after a recognized heart attack, 35 percent of women will have another heart attack, 14 percent will develop angina (chest pain), 11 percent will have a stroke, 6 percent will die, and 46 percent will develop heart failure.[8]

What is the reason for such a difference between women and men? It may be that the message is more forcefully delivered to men to reduce heart-disease risks (i.e., to quit smoking, manage cholesterol, control hypertension and diabetes), while women hear more about the risks of breast cancer. We find that women do not go to the doctor until later in life, when they have already developed unstable angina or are having a heart attack. When they are diagnosed with heart disease, they generally have more advanced disease, intervention is both riskier and more difficult, and they are more likely than men to die from heart disease.

## Signs and Symptoms of Heart Disease in Women

Another reason for the increase in CVD-related deaths in women is illustrated in Ruth's and Bernie's harrowing experiences with heart disease. Signs and symptoms of heart problems are less specific in women and can be easily overlooked. Women and their doctors may be "faked out" by atypical symptoms of heart disease, which contributes to a delay in diagnosis.

The following chart compares the gender differences related to heart-attack symptoms.[9]

## Gender Differences in Symptoms of Heart Attack

| MEN'S SYMPTOMS | WOMEN'S SYMPTOMS |
|---|---|
| Chest pain or pressure | Pain in chest, upper back, jaw, or neck |
| Pain while resting | Shortness of breath |
| Pain down left arm and shoulder | Flulike symptoms: nausea, vomiting, cold sweats |
| Weakness | Fatigue or weakness |
| | Feeling of anxiety, loss of appetite, malaise |

A recent study gives further insight into how women experience heart attacks. Five hundred female heart-attack survivors were surveyed, and 95 percent of them experienced new and different physical symptoms up to one month before their attacks. Fatigue and sleeping problems topped the list. It is interesting to note that 43 percent of these patients reported no chest pain before having their heart attacks, and those who did report it described the sensation as pressure, aching, or tightness instead of specific pain.

The most common symptoms reported were:

- Unexplained or unusual fatigue (71 percent)
- Sleep disturbance (48 percent)
- Shortness of breath (42 percent)
- Indigestion (39 percent)
- Anxiety (35 percent)[10]

You can see how someone like Ruth might dismiss her symptoms as being related to flu, fatigue, stress, aging, or just a hectic lifestyle. This study raises a red flag for women to pay attention to their bodies and be aware of signs or symptoms that could indicate heart problems. If you have a sudden onset of unusual symptoms, experience a change of symptoms, or just don't feel well, you should see your doctor.

## Heart Health Risks in Women

Another difference between women and men when it comes to heart disease relates to the outcome after heart surgery. More than five hundred thousand coronary artery bypass graft (CABG) procedures—in layperson's terms, bypass surgeries—are performed in this country every year. More than 150,000 of them are performed on women. As a rule, women fare worse than men with respect to the seriousness of CVD (morbidity) and death rate (mortality).[11]

There are several reasons for this, some of which are fairly obvious. First, compared to men, women generally are shorter, weigh less, and have a smaller body surface area. This means women generally have smaller coronary arteries, which are more readily clogged than the larger arteries in men. And the smaller size of women's coronary arteries presents a greater technical challenge for performing angioplasty or bypass surgery. Second, because estrogen is thought to provide a protective effect against cardiovascular disease, women are rarely affected by CVD before menopause. As such, most women are older and in worse overall physical condition when they do require treatment. Finally, women are also more likely to have the complications of "co-morbid" conditions, including diabetes, high blood pressure, congestive heart failure, obesity, and cerebral or peripheral vascular disease (disease that restricts circulation to the brain or extremities).[12]

In addition to gender-related risks, there are a number of other factors that can lead to cardiovascular disease in both women and men. These are called risk factors. Risk factors are divided into two categories: major and contributing. The major risk factors are those that have been proved to increase the risk of heart disease. Contributing factors are those that doctors think can lead to an increased risk, but the exact role they play may not be defined.

Only one of the major risk factors is not preventable: family history. In the study of five hundred postinfarction women, an astounding 96 percent had a family history of heart disease.[13] However, four risk factors for heart disease are largely preventable through diet, exercise, and lifestyle. Here are six of the major risk factors with a brief explanation of each.

## Smoking

Cigarette smoking has been medically determined to be a major risk factor for coronary artery disease (CAD). Smoking is generally linked to a more severe form of atherosclerosis than that which occurs from poor diet. Smokers have at least a 200 percent greater risk of developing coronary heart disease than nonsmokers. Smoking causes a variety of adverse physical responses that result in accelerated production of plaque in the coronary arteries (hardening of the arteries). Increased plaque also heightens the risk of blood clots, which cause heart attacks. Smoking has also been shown to increase LDL (bad cholesterol) and decrease HDL (good cholesterol). We can't say this too strongly: *smoking will kill your heart; don't smoke!*

## High Cholesterol

Hyperlipidemia refers to a high level of fats circulating in the bloodstream. Cholesterol is one of the groups that make up the fatty or lipid compounds in the bloodstream. Most cholesterol is transported to the body's cells in small particles called low-density lipoprotein (LDL). High levels of LDL are associated with increased risk for heart disease, earning it the designation of "bad cholesterol." When LDL levels are high, resulting from a diet of high-cholesterol foods, they deposit on the walls of the arteries as plaque. Over a period of time, the plaque can cause obstruction or occlusion of an artery, triggering a heart attack.

## Diabetes

Diabetes, categorized as Type I and Type II, is a disease in which the body cannot process sugar—glucose—in the normal fashion. Type I diabetes, also called insulin-dependent, child-onset, or juvenile diabetes, results when the pancreas no longer produces insulin, which is necessary for the body to process glucose from the blood to the cells. Type I diabetes patients must receive regular insulin injections to live.

Type II diabetes, also called non-insulin-dependent or adult-onset diabetes, results when the pancreas does not produce enough insulin or the cells in the body ignore the insulin. When glucose builds up in the bloodstream instead of going into the cells, your cells may become starved for energy. Over time, high blood-glucose levels can cause kidney disease, blindness, atherosclerosis, and heart disease.

An alarming 6 percent of the U.S. population (15.7 million people) have diabetes, and this reality cannot be dismissed as wholly congenital. Cultural environment—such as the bad information about food and consumption we get on TV—and personal behavior—such as overeating and too much fat in the diet—are primarily at fault in the soaring numbers of adult diabetes patients.

Persons with diabetes also tend to have other traits that make them more at risk for developing heart problems. These include obesity, a sedentary lifestyle, high blood pressure, and high cholesterol. Forty percent of women who have cardiovascular events, such as heart attack or stroke, also have diabetes.

## Hypertension

Hypertension is the medical term for high blood pressure. The American Heart Association estimates that more than fifty million Americans suffer from hypertension, including one of every four adults. Hypertension is the leading cause of stroke and a major risk factor for heart attack and kidney failure. There are no typical symptoms for hypertension, so without periodic blood pressure screenings, you may be unaware of its presence.

## Obesity

Obesity is defined as a body mass index greater than 30. Body mass index will be more fully explained in chapter 8. Obesity has been directly associated with increased risk of heart disease, including hypertension, hyperlipidemia, diabetes, and vascular disease. Weight reduction for obese persons significantly decreases these problems and therefore lowers the risk of developing coronary heart disease.

## Family History

Jackie led a very active life, thoroughly involved in homeschooling her children and leading women's Bible studies at her church. One day as she was preparing dinner, with her two kids and her best friend in the kitchen, Jackie suddenly dropped to the floor like a stone. One minute this forty-five-year-old was vibrant, animated, and busy; the next moment she was dead—just that quick. An autopsy revealed a congenital heart condition that had never surfaced in her medical history. Her heart simply gave out without warning. A careful look at her family background uncovered the early sudden death of her grandfather, who died before Jackie was born.

Some forms of heart disease are inherited from family members, and some, like Jackie's, may lie undetected until it is too late. *If you have a family history of heart disease, particularly in your parents, it is important that you see your doctor regularly to monitor your physical condition.* Even without a known background of heart problems in your family, you are wise to take advantage of all preventive measures to keep your heart healthy, including periodic physical exams, a healthy diet, and regular exercise.

Heart disease is your physical heart's number one enemy. In this book, we will give you solid medical counsel on how you can guard your physical heart and maximize your opportunity to live a long, quality life by taking good care of your heart. We join Dr. Ed and Jo Beth Young in urging you to make a commitment to a Total Heart Health lifestyle, both for yourself and for your family.

Your spiritual heart is also under assault and in need of proactive care. In the next chapter, Dr. and Mrs. Young will talk about spiritual heart disease, how to avoid it, and how to find healing from it.

# Keys to Total Heart Health

## Chapter 6: Heart Health— A Real Life-and-Death Matter

- Cardiovascular disease (CVD) is the number one health threat to women and the leading cause of death in the United States and the Western world.

- Most women are unaware of the seriousness of the problem.

- Heart disease increases proportionately in women in every age group up into the sixties.

- The incidence of CVD-related deaths is *decreasing* in men but *increasing* in women.

- The most common symptoms up to one month before a heart attack reported by women are unexplained or unusual fatigue, sleep disturbance, shortness of breath, indigestion, and anxiety.

- More than 150,000 bypass surgeries are performed on women annually in the United States, and women fare worse than men with respect to CVD and death rate.

- Of the major risk factors for CVD, only one is not preventable: family history. The rest include smoking, high cholesterol, diabetes, hypertension, and obesity.

# 7
# Resist the Assault
# on Your Spiritual Heart

Turn from fear and resignation,
and your life will light up with hope.

**Ed and Jo Beth Young**

The heartwarming story of Mary Kay Beard has been an inspiration to me (Jo Beth) and to thousands of other women. It's a story of great hope for healing a hurting spiritual heart.

Mary Kay's future loomed as gray and empty as the grim prison cell that defined her tiny world. Years earlier in Missouri, this young woman who had excelled as a student and impressed everyone with her wit and promise was seduced. Her heart was drawn away from decency by the allure of possessions and crime.

Mary Kay loved sparkling jewels, luxurious furs, and the lifestyle that surrounded them. The fastest way to acquire all the things she wanted was not the right way. But crime brought her cash, and cash allowed her to buy the treasures for which she yearned. Migrating to the southeastern United States, she and her male partner earned the nickname "the Bonnie and Clyde of Alabama" for their extended crime spree.

But the fast track to riches eventually became a dead end. Mary Kay was arrested by the FBI in Alabama for burglary, grand larceny, and robbery and was sentenced to twenty-two years in prison. Her drab prison garb was a far cry from the finery she had enjoyed. Sadness and despair overwhelmed her. During those first few weeks in prison, she resigned herself to a hopeless existence.

As the years began to pass, however, Mary Kay decided to make the best of her situation. She entered an education-completion program through the prison system. But the most important education she received was about God. Through the ministry of Christian women who came to the prison to lead church services, Mary Kay gave her life to Christ. As her new spiritual life began to emerge, Mary Kay found windows opening in the walls of her prison. The cold stone was still there, but she could finally see hope for her life, for both the present and the future.

Mary Kay became as fascinated with unlocking the Bible's secrets as she had once been with cracking a safe. Her spiritual growth was rapid, and soon she was teaching others. And then a miracle happened. Mary Kay was released from prison after serving only six years of her sentence.

After her release, Mary Kay could not forget the people she had left behind in prison. One year later she was appointed Alabama director for Prison Fellowship, the organization founded by Chuck Colson. Mary Kay remembered the lonely Christmases she had spent in prison. She recalled how inmates who received gifts of toiletries from local churches would rewrap the small treasures in scraps of cloth and paper to give to their own children for Christmas. Mary Kay's compassion for inmates and their children sparked an idea that was destined to brighten the holidays for inmates and their families around the country for years to come.

As the Christmas season approached in 1982, Mary Kay convinced shopping malls in Birmingham and Montgomery to put up special Christmas trees to benefit the children of inmates. Shoppers were encouraged to buy gifts for the "wish lists" of the children and leave them under the Christmas trees. Throughout the area, these mall trees were soon bedecked with gifts. Mary Kay and her crew then distributed the gifts through Christmas parties at local churches. That first year, 556 Alabama children received gifts through what has become known as "Angel Tree."

In the years that followed, Mary Kay Beard's compassionate dream spread across the country. More than five million children of prison inmates have received Christmas gifts through Angel Tree. In one year alone, more than thirteen thousand churches participated in this ministry of love and hope. Thanks to God's grace, Mary Kay Beard broke out of the hopelessness that imprisoned her heart, allowing her to find joy and freedom in an impossible situation and to share these gifts with others.

Just as the ravages of cardiovascular disease can cripple and kill the physical heart, so a sense of hopelessness and resignation can imprison the spiritual heart. The enemy of your heart would like nothing better than to weaken you to the point of ineffectiveness in your service to Christ, your family, your church, and the needy world around you. And being a sly, conniving thief, he will work in the shadows to exploit any spiritual or emotional weakness in order to infect your heart with disabling disease. When you are bowed down under fear and resignation, you will feel worthless to yourself, to God, and to others. And that's just where the devil wants you.

What are the signs of spiritual disease encroaching on a woman's heart? Edwin and I want to share with you five risk factors that promote a sagging spiritual heart and how Jesus Christ can help you confront and neutralize their threat and live with renewed hope and expectation.

## Confronting Negative Family History

Carole grew up in a non-Christian home with a mother who smothered her with criticism. No matter what Carole did, her mom always found a way to ignore the right and good things while castigating her for her mistakes. It grieved the little girl that she could not please her mother, causing her to work even harder to meet her mom's unreal expectations. At age nine, Carole began attending Sunday school with a neighborhood friend and opened her heart to God's love. But little changed at home. She continued to live under the cloud of her mother's disapproval.

Now in her early forties, Carole is still trying to please her mother. In her head, she understands that the environment she grew up in was dysfunctional. And she knows that her mom has simply lived out the negativism and disapproval she experienced as a child with her own parents. But in her heart, Carole still yearns for words of acceptance and approval from a mother who seems unable to give it. She approaches every visit to her mom's home with fragile hope that she can say or do something that will evoke a smile or "Thank you, Carole." But she always goes home hurt and in tears. Even with a loving husband and numerous supportive, affirming friends, Carole feels locked in a cell of hopelessness.

As Drs. Duncan and Leachman have explained, your family health history is one of the primary determinants for your physical health. If your parents were victims of some form of cardiovascular disease, you are at greater risk to encounter similar problems and must be doubly careful to guard your heart. And for those unfortunate enough to inherit a propensity for heart disease, there is not much you can do about changing it.

Similarly, when it comes to the spiritual heart, heredity can also deal you a potentially losing hand. Like Carole, you may have grown up in a home where you were robbed of parental acceptance and approval. Your heart may bear the scars of any number of difficulties in your growing-up family: physical, sexual, or emotional abuse; alcoholism; divorce; poverty; occult activity; abandonment; and so on. Even as a Christian, you may feel shackled to your dysfunctional past because emotional and spiritual heredity has such a tight grip on your heart.

Unlike physical heredity, you *can* do something about your spiritual heredity. The key to overcoming a painful family history is to focus on who you *are* instead of who you *were*. The woman dominated by the old life lives in "I was-ness." But God is always "I Am," and those restored to the Father are empowered to live in "I Am-ness."

No matter how your spirit was stifled or stunted in the past, if you are a child of God, you have been adopted into a new family spiritually. God is your Father now, and He accepts you unconditionally because of what Jesus Christ did on the cross. Paul wrote, "Those who become Christians become new persons. They are not the same anymore, for the old life is gone. A new life has begun!" (2 Corinthians 5:17 NLT). Your life is in the hands of One who will never abuse you, ignore you, abandon you, or fail you. Whenever you are haunted by hurts from the past, begin to praise God for who you are in Christ. And if a painful upbringing has stunted your progress in following God, we encourage you to seek wise counsel to help you work through your difficult issues.

## Confronting Spiritual Neglect

A young man went off to college. "Promise me one thing," his mother said before he left home. "Promise me you will be in church every Sunday." This loving son promised he would do what she asked.

At college, one of the boy's new friends invited him to his family's ranch for a weekend. On Saturday evening, the host said, "Tomorrow we're going to ride horses to the lake and fish all day." On Sunday morning, as they rode out, our young friend heard the peal of a church bell in the distance, but he nudged his horse onward. Again the bell sounded, but this time fainter. The young man kept riding. The third time, the bell was barely audible. Suddenly, this college freshman turned his horse around and started riding back.

"Where are you going?" his host asked.

The young man replied, "I have to turn back while I can still hear the bell." God never ceases to call to us and offer us His strength for our hearts. But life's activities, demands, and distractions can draw us out of the range of the bell, and we begin to lose our heart, our passion for God and life. Don't neglect the bell while you can still hear it!

In Proverbs 1:24–25, wisdom—which is equated with the fear of the Lord—speaks: "I called and you refused, I stretched out my hand and no one paid attention; and you neglected all my counsel and did not want my reproof." The Hebrew word translated "counsel" means plans or strategies. God will help us overcome spiritual heart disease if we heed His strategies. But if we neglect Him and wander far from His call, the sad payoff will be "calamity," "dread," "distress," and "anguish" (vv. 26–27).

## Confronting Poor Spiritual Diet

Tracy, who has been a Christian since childhood, can't understand why she is so weak when resisting temptation. She owns half a dozen versions of the Bible, which are wedged into a vast library of Christian romance novels, sermon tapes, and Christian music CDs in her bookcase. Whenever she has time, Tracy tunes in to the most popular religious programs on TV and radio because she feels better when she listens to the music and the talks. Yet when the pressure is on in her life, Tracy always feels spiritually anemic.

Tracy suffers from the same problem the Christians in the city of Corinth suffered from two thousand years ago. In 1 Corinthians 3, Paul lamented that the church at Corinth could stomach only spiritual milk when he wanted to serve them meat. They were spiritual babies when they should have been more mature. That was Tracy's problem. She invested a lot of her free time in reading Christian novels and listening to music, sermons, and programs that gave her a religious "buzz." She was getting a lot to "eat" spiritually, but most of it was "milk." Her approach to Bible study was a mile wide and an inch deep. No wonder she lacked the resources to withstand temptation.

We all know the health risks of eating too much fast food—high calories, high fat, low nutritional value. Trying to stay alive on "fast faith" like Tracy's instead of regular, substantial feeding on the Word of God will leave your spiritual heart malnourished, weak, and vulnerable. God asks His people, "Why do you spend money for what is not bread, and your wages for what does not satisfy?" (Isaiah 55:2). He's talking about spiritual food here. The solution to this problem is in the same verse: "Listen carefully to Me, and eat what is good, and delight yourself in abundance."

Jesus said, "I am the Bread of Life. The person who aligns with me hungers no more and thirsts no more, ever" (John 6:36 MSG). It is vital to the health and strength of your spiritual heart that you feed consistently on Christ and His Word through purposeful Bible study and prayer. We will talk more about formulating a healthy spiritual diet in chapter 15.

## Confronting the Sedentary Life

Another side of Tracy's problem is a lack of spiritual exercise. Not only is she not eating enough lean spiritual meat, but she isn't exercising her faith. She attends church, reads books, and listens to tapes to get something for herself. But she is doing little in ministry for others. She's a spiritual couch potato; she doesn't "work out" her salvation through deliberate acts of service (see Philippians 2:12). As a result, she has little spiritual muscle for her ongoing warfare against temptation.

Our two heart doctors will be talking about the importance of energy balance for a healthy physical heart. You need a good balance between the energy you take in—food—and the energy you expend—physical activity and exercise. For most of us, our energy is out of balance; we take in too much and expend too little. The result is that more than half of our population is clinically overweight, which leads to all kinds of physical problems.

Energy balance is just as important to spiritual vitality. We need "energy in"—a healthy spiritual diet of Bible reading, prayer, and worship—and we need "energy out"—a disciplined approach to serving God and others through activities of helpfulness. Too little spiritual exercise, and you get spiritually flabby. It's important to keep in shape and develop good muscle tone by staying spiritually active. Find ways to use your unique abilities to display God's love and help others in your church and community. We will share much more about spiritual "energy out" in chapter 17.

## Confronting Fear of Failure

Another debilitating ailment threatening the health of a woman's spiritual heart is the fear of failure. Growth and change are part of life. We are works of art in progress. Cherish your opportunities to keep learning, maturing, and expanding your borders as a follower of Christ. Even the apostle Paul recognized that he had not "arrived" at complete spiritual perfection or maturity; he was a work in progress. He wrote of his ongoing development in Christ, "Forgetting what lies behind and reaching forward to what lies ahead, I press on toward the goal for the prize of the upward call of God in Christ Jesus" (Philippians 3:13–14).

Your spiritual heart has limitless growth potential. Indeed, if your spiritual heart isn't in a growth mode, it is in danger of atrophying. But growth isn't easy. In Paul's words, it requires reaching forward and pressing onward. These words picture a race in which the competitors are sprinting, stretching, and straining toward the tape in order to win the gold medal.

The problem is that a lot of Christians never leave the starting line. They don't want to grow because they are afraid they will fail. Or they start into the race and give up because there are too many obstacles or disappointments. They say things like, "I've tried this before and it didn't work," or "I'm going to fall flat on my face and look like a fool," or "I'm just not good enough, so why try?"

If you have ever experienced a setback or a disappointment as a Christian, you know what we mean. Every year you vow to read through the Bible, but you've never made it past Job. You tried to start a neighborhood Bible study group in your home, but nobody came. You want family Bible reading to be meaningful to your kids, but every attempt is a joke to them. A non-Christian at the gym snubbed you after you shared your faith with her, so you aren't ready to try that again. You compare your meager efforts for Christ with the accomplishments of other Christian women you know, and you say, "I'm nothing." Or perhaps a sinful past mocks any attempt at moving forward with Christ.

One of the keys to overcoming your fear of failure and moving forward toward a stronger spiritual heart is to *not* look backward. Paul said, "Forgetting what lies behind . . ." In this race, everybody trips and falls occasionally. Everybody makes a wrong turn. Everybody pulls up lame. Everybody "hits the wall" with fatigue. The idea is not to run without mistakes; the idea is to stay in the race and finish well. Every woman who perseveres and finishes gets a gold medal. When you hit an obstacle or experience failure, you just leave it in the past, focus on the finish line, and keep going.

Donna Rice has done exactly that. Years ago, Donna was a member of the South Carolina church where we served. We watched her grow up to become a vivacious young professional woman and aspiring actress. Her life took many twists and turns over the years, but we didn't know how far Donna had drifted from her dynamic commitment to Christ until the searing media spotlight exposed her at the center of a national sex scandal. In 1987, presidential hopeful Senator Gary Hart was reportedly having an affair with Donna, ending his quest for the White House.

"Donna, what happened next?" we asked her years later. She told of going underground for seven years, purposely retreating from the media glare. "I was desperate," she said. "I thought my life was over and that I'd never have credibility again. I was hounded by the press everywhere I went." Donna was offered millions of dollars to tell her life story and to pose for men's magazines. She turned them all down.

Donna determined not to go the way of other women caught in sexual snares. She received God's forgiveness, renewed her commitment to Christ, and began moving forward. Eventually Donna became one of America's strongest advocates for Internet safety as president of an organization dedicated to protecting children and families from pornography.

"What turned you around?" we asked Donna one day. She took us all the way back to a Sunday in Columbia, South Carolina. Young Donna had brought a friend to church, and that woman accepted Christ. Eventually Donna's friend went to seminary to prepare herself for full-time ministry.

When Donna stalled in her spiritual growth and got into trouble, that friend she had brought to church years earlier sent her an audiotape. "Donna, God loves you," she said. "You know you have Jesus Christ in your life. He will give you a fresh start. He will let you begin again."

Donna Rice had fallen flat on her face as a Christian. But she didn't wallow in her failure or use it as an excuse to fear the future. Forgetting what was behind, Donna dealt with her failure and allowed Jesus to pull her up and get her back in the race. Had she yielded to fear of another failure, she would have forfeited the growth in Christ she has enjoyed, and the world would have suffered for lack of what God has done through her in the fight against pornography.

If you hope to successfully confront and neutralize the risk factors for spiritual heart disease, you need to be a woman of hope. Often we think of hope as a wish for something to happen. For example, you enter your name in an Internet sweepstakes hoping—wishing—you will win the prize of a $5,000 shopping spree. The problem is, there may be millions of people wishing and hoping for the same thing, and only one person's hopes will be realized.

That's not the kind of hope we're talking about. The New Testament word translated "hope" means to anticipate a desired outcome with expectation. If God has promised it, if God is the power behind it, you don't have to wish for it—because it's going to happen. In Texas-speak, we say, "It's a done deal."

Has God promised you success in the journey to spiritual maturity? Yes. Does He take primary responsibility for the health of your spiritual heart? Absolutely! Paul exclaimed, "There has never been the slightest doubt in my mind that the God who started this great work in you would keep at it and bring it to a flourishing finish on the very day Christ Jesus appears" (Philippians 1:6 MSG). God is the One who got you out of the starting blocks and into the race in the first place in response to your faith in Christ. And He is on the track with you now, empowering you by the Holy Spirit to keep reaching forward. You simply must cooperate with His plan for finishing the race. What can you do to cooperate? We'll be talking more about that in part 3.

Even if your walk with Christ has been severely hindered by one or more of the risk factors we have mentioned, don't give up the race. It's not too late. Grab hold of God's hope-filled promises, and run to win.

The health of your spiritual heart and your physical heart depends on what you feed them. In the next two chapters, Drs. Duncan and Leachman will unmask one of the primary enemies of the physical heart: the problem of eating too much.

# Keys to Total Heart Health

## Chapter 7: Resist the Assault on Your Spiritual Heart

- Just as the ravages of cardiovascular disease can cripple and kill the physical heart, so a sense of hopelessness and resignation can imprison the spiritual heart.
- Signs of spiritual heart disease:
  1. *Family history.* While you may not be able to do anything about physical heredity, you can do something about your spiritual heredity by accepting your new life in Christ.
  2. *Spiritual neglect.* God will help you overcome spiritual heart disease if you heed His strategies, but neglect will lead to worry and distress.
  3. *Poor spiritual diet.* Trying to stay alive on "fast faith" rather than substantial feeding on the Word of God will leave your spiritual heart malnourished.
  4. *Lack of spiritual exercise.* Energy balance—energy in, energy out—is just as important to spiritual vitality as to physical vitality. Find ways to serve God by serving others.
  5. *Fear of failure.* One of the keys to overcoming your fear of failure and moving forward toward a stronger spiritual heart is to *not* look backward.
- If you hope to successfully neutralize the risk factors for spiritual heart disease, you need to be a woman of hope.

# 8

# Are You Eating to Live or Living to Eat?

The path to a healthy physical heart
goes through your stomach.

**Dr. Michael Duncan and Dr. Richard Leachman**

Like a lot of women today, Toni leads a fast-paced life. She works thirty-two hours a week as a dental office billing clerk, she's the wife of a video-store manager, and she's the mother of two boys and a girl, ages eleven to fourteen. The kids are in sports most of the year, so Toni runs the family shuttle service to and from soccer, baseball, or basketball practice just about every day after she leaves her office at three o'clock. And when she *is* home, there is laundry to fold and a house to keep tidy.

Most days, planning a menu and cooking dinner are the last things Toni wants to think about. Besides, puttering in the kitchen is not something she really enjoys, and many evenings she and the kids are in the minivan or at a game at dinnertime. And Bob doesn't usually get home until after eight.

So convenience and speed are the key elements for the evening meal. That often means drive-through burgers, fried chicken, pizza, or tacos on the way home from sports. Or everyone picks out frozen meals at home and takes turns nuking them in the microwave. On Sundays after church, the family goes out to a nice sit-down restaurant for a big lunch. And there are always fast-food leftovers in the fridge for anyone who gets hungry between meals.

Toni's family doesn't care much for her cooking when she does cook—and neither does she. So everyone seems happy with the way they do dinner. Toni has a weight problem and chides herself about eating too much. But after a busy day she is really hungry, and she loves the food at their favorite eating places. So a more sensible eating plan—and losing extra pounds—is always in the future.

Connie is a single career woman living alone. She leaves the house every morning by six thirty, picks up a grande double-shot espresso at the corner coffee shop, and starts work in her office by seven thirty. The word *breakfast* isn't in her vocabulary. She drinks coffee until ten and then visits the vending machines in the lobby for chips or cookies to tide her over until lunch.

Eating out most days at noon with coworkers, Connie usually orders a big salad with low-fat dressing. Her friends razz her for eating so sensibly. But by midafternoon she's back to the vending machines for snacks and soda. Dinner at home is often a bowl of healthy soup with rice cakes. While working at her computer or watching TV in the evening, she rewards herself for good meal choices with a sweet treat: a bowl of ice cream or a slice of pie.

Connie wants to shed about ten pounds. She reasons that eating only two meals a day—healthy meals at that—should do the trick. But she stays within a pound or two of what she has weighed for months. In her thinking, between-meal snacks are helping her from overeating at mealtimes—and besides: they're only *snacks*. Her nightly desserts are viewed as rewards for eating sensibly at lunch and dinner. Connie is comfortable eating this way, and if she has to choose, she'll live with the extra weight.

## Eat, Drink, and Be Merry?

One of the most insidious lies perpetrated against the human heart today centers on food. And like most lies, this one is a subtle perversion of the truth. God designed the human body in such a way that we must *eat to live*. We cannot operate without fuel—the air we breathe and the food and liquids we consume. The tragedy of anorexia in our culture demonstrates what happens when someone refuses to eat. But our culture is bombarded today with the twisted, appealing, and convincing message that we must *live to eat*. And the difference in how these three little words are arranged can literally kill you.

By God's marvelous design, if you eat the right kinds of foods in appropriate quantities, you will maximize your opportunities to live a long, healthy, and productive life. You can work into your sixties or seventies if you want and still have a couple of decades for the fun of retirement. Make plans to dance at the weddings of your grandchildren—maybe even your great-grandchildren! All you have to do is keep your heart humming along at maximum efficiency with the right fuel and care.

But it is difficult to maintain a sane eat-to-live program in a food-crazed, live-to-eat society. Enjoyment in life is so often equated with food—good food, rich food, piles of food. The employee at the fast-food counter asks, "Would you like to super-size your meal for only fifty cents more?" Food ads on TV push taste, convenience, quantity, and value (more calories and fat for less money) over nutrition. The ads and coupons for the supermarket tempt us to plan weekly menus based on what's on sale instead of what's healthy for our family.

Quantity is the most common problem for women today regarding food. When you eat, your body turns the food into energy and then burns that energy through your daily activity. When you put more fuel energy into your system than you can immediately use, your body holds the residual in ready reserve and uses it if fuel intake is low. But when you consistently take in more fuel than you burn and your reserves are full, the body must find a place to store the excess. Medically speaking, that storage facility is called adipose tissue, which is located throughout your body. In unflattering layperson's terms, this tissue my be described as "saddlebags" or "thunder thighs." That's right, we're talking about fat.

A healthy body burns fuel and stores fuel in reserve. The main form of fuel storage in the body is fat. For the typical 125-pound woman, roughly 20 percent of body weight—about twenty-five pounds—is fat. Statistically, most of us carry more than that. Fuel storage assures that you will be able to survive and function for a time even when you are unable to eat or choose not to eat through a fast. But excessive fuel storage over the long haul taxes the body, precipitates disease, and shortens life.

The live-to-eat perversion in our country has reached epidemic proportions. We are experiencing a medical crisis that is literally killing us. The epidemic is obesity, the sad and dangerous result of falling prey to the live-to-eat lie in our culture. Obesity is the most common metabolic disorder in the Western world. The American Obesity Association Web site reports that 64.5 percent of adult Americans (about 127 million) are categorized as being overweight or obese.[1] Furthermore, sixty million Americans are clinically obese, and nine million are severely obese.[2]

## Body Mass Index: How Much Is Too Much?

One of the helpful tools for determining how much weight is too much is called the body mass index (BMI). Years of obesity research have helped us determine a healthy range for a person's weight in proportion to her height. Simply put, your height is a reliable standard for determining how much you can weigh and still be within the margin of good health.

You calculate BMI using the following formula:
your weight in pounds
divided by your height in inches squared
multiplied by a factor of 703

For example, let's calculate the BMI of two women with the same weight. Alicia stands 5'10" (70 inches) and weighs 170 pounds.

Alicia's height in inches squared (70 x 70) equals 4,900.
Her weight in pounds (170) divided by 4,900 equals 0.035.
0.035 times 703 equals a BMI of 24.6.

Barb also weighs 170 pounds but is only 5'3" tall.

Barb's height in inches squared (63 x 63) equals 3,969.
Her weight in pounds (170) divided by 3,969 equals 0.043.
0.043 times 703 equals a BMI of 30.2.

*Overweight* is clinically defined as a body mass index of 25 or greater. *Obesity* is clinically defined as a BMI of 30 or greater. A BMI of 40 or greater indicates *severe obesity*, also called *morbid obesity*. Numerous studies have shown that a BMI above 25 increases a person's risk of dying early, mainly from heart disease and cancer. Conversely, death rates decline when the BMI is within the safe range.

Alicia, with a BMI just under 25, is inside the safe range, just short of being overweight for her height. Barb's BMI of 30.2 puts her in the obesity range and at higher risk than Alicia for heart disease, related problems, and earlier death. The chart below will help you quickly identify the weight range that is safe for your height.

## Tipping the Scales: A National Epidemic

It is sobering to note that the prevalence of clinically overweight and obese persons in our country has increased dramatically during the past three decades and especially in the last several years. This disturbing and dangerous trend has affected all age groups of both genders, as the following tables prepared by the American Obesity Association indicate.

| Height (in.) | Weight (lb.) | | | | | | | | | | | | | |
|---|---|---|---|---|---|---|---|---|---|---|---|---|---|---|
| 58 | 91 | 96 | 100 | 105 | 110 | 115 | 119 | 124 | 129 | 134 | 138 | 143 | 167 | 191 |
| 59 | 94 | 99 | 104 | 109 | 114 | 119 | 124 | 128 | 133 | 138 | 143 | 148 | 173 | 198 |
| 60 | 97 | 102 | 107 | 112 | 118 | 123 | 128 | 133 | 138 | 143 | 148 | 153 | 179 | 204 |
| 61 | 100 | 106 | 111 | 116 | 122 | 127 | 132 | 137 | 143 | 148 | 153 | 158 | 185 | 211 |
| 62 | 104 | 109 | 115 | 120 | 126 | 131 | 136 | 142 | 147 | 153 | 158 | 164 | 191 | 218 |
| 63 | 107 | 113 | 118 | 124 | 130 | 135 | 141 | 146 | 152 | 158 | 163 | 169 | 197 | 225 |
| 64 | 110 | 116 | 122 | 128 | 134 | 140 | 145 | 151 | 157 | 163 | 169 | 174 | 204 | 232 |
| 65 | 114 | 120 | 126 | 132 | 138 | 144 | 150 | 156 | 162 | 168 | 174 | 180 | 210 | 240 |
| 66 | 118 | 124 | 130 | 136 | 142 | 148 | 155 | 161 | 167 | 173 | 179 | 186 | 216 | 247 |
| 67 | 121 | 127 | 134 | 140 | 146 | 153 | 159 | 166 | 172 | 178 | 185 | 191 | 223 | 255 |
| 68 | 125 | 131 | 138 | 144 | 151 | 158 | 164 | 171 | 177 | 184 | 190 | 197 | 230 | 262 |
| 69 | 128 | 135 | 142 | 149 | 155 | 162 | 169 | 176 | 182 | 189 | 196 | 203 | 236 | 270 |
| 70 | 132 | 139 | 146 | 153 | 160 | 167 | 174 | 181 | 188 | 195 | 202 | 207 | 243 | 276 |
| 71 | 136 | 143 | 150 | 157 | 165 | 172 | 179 | 186 | 193 | 200 | 208 | 215 | 250 | 286 |
| 72 | 140 | 147 | 154 | 162 | 169 | 177 | 184 | 191 | 199 | 206 | 213 | 221 | 258 | 294 |
| 73 | 144 | 151 | 159 | 166 | 174 | 182 | 189 | 197 | 204 | 212 | 219 | 227 | 265 | 302 |
| 74 | 148 | 155 | 163 | 171 | 179 | 186 | 194 | 202 | 210 | 218 | 225 | 233 | 272 | 311 |
| 75 | 152 | 160 | 168 | 176 | 184 | 192 | 200 | 208 | 216 | 224 | 232 | 240 | 279 | 319 |
| 76 | 156 | 164 | 172 | 180 | 189 | 197 | 205 | 213 | 221 | 230 | 238 | 246 | 287 | 328 |
| BMI | 19 | 20 | 21 | 22 | 23 | 24 | 25 | 26 | 27 | 28 | 29 | 30 | 35 | 40 |

The first table (below) reports the rise in the number of overweight, obese, and severely obese men and women between two statistical periods: 1988–1994 and 1999–2000. For example, you can see that the prevalence of overweight women in the United States rose from 51.2 percent to 62 percent between the two periods, indicating that 62 percent of all American women in 1999–2000 were clinically overweight.[3]

| | Men Prevalence (%) | | Women Prevalence (%) | |
| --- | --- | --- | --- | --- |
| | 1988–1994 | 1999–2000 | 1988–1994 | 1999–2000 |
| **Overweight** BMI 25 or greater | 61 | 67 | 51.2 | 62 |
| **Obese** BMI 30 or greater | 20.6 | 27.7 | 26 | 34 |
| **Severely Obese** BMI 40 or greater | 1.7 | 3.12 | 4 | 6.3 |

The second table breaks down the rise in overweight prevalence into age categories for men and women. Note, for example, that 63.6 percent of women ages thirty-five to forty-four were overweight in 1999–2000 as compared to 49.6 percent in 1988–1994—an increase of 14 percentage points.[4]

## Overweight (BMI 25 or greater)

| Age (Years) | Men Prevalence (%) | | Women Prevalence (%) | |
|---|---|---|---|---|
| | 1988–1994 | 1999–2000 | 1988–1994 | 1999–2000 |
| 22–34 | 47.5 | 58.0 | 37.0 | 51.5 |
| 35–44 | 65.5 | 67.6 | 49.6 | 63.6 |
| 45–54 | 66.1 | 71.3 | 60.3 | 64.7 |
| 55–64 | 70.5 | 72.5 | 66.3 | 73.1 |
| 65–74 | 68.5 | 77.2 | 60.3 | 70.1 |
| 75+ | 56.5 | 66.4 | 52.3 | 59.6 |

The third table (below) reflects the increase in prevalence of obesity between the two statistical periods by age groups. Notice that nearly 12 percent more women ages sixty-five to seventy-four were clinically obese in 1999–2000 than in 1988–1994.[5]

## Obese (BMI 30 or greater)

| Age (Years) | Men Prevalence (%) | | Women Prevalence (%) | |
|---|---|---|---|---|
| | 1988–1994 | 1999–2000 | 1988–1994 | 1999–2000 |
| 22–34 | 14.1 | 24.1 | 18.5 | 25.8 |
| 35–44 | 21.5 | 25.2 | 25.5 | 33.9 |
| 45–54 | 23.2 | 30.1 | 32.4 | 38.1 |
| 55–64 | 27.2 | 32.9 | 33.7 | 43.1 |
| 65–74 | 24.1 | 33.4 | 26.9 | 38.8 |
| 75+ | 13.2 | 20.4 | 19.2 | 25.1 |

In the U.S. alone, three hundred thousand deaths annually are directly related to obesity, costing an estimated $100 billion.[6] This deadly rise has occurred despite all the information about the dangers of being overweight and obese. No, we don't see boldly printed warnings from the surgeon general on hamburger wrappers, ice-cream cartons, and menus at the doughnut shop like we do on cigarette packs. But who hasn't been informed or sternly warned by someone in the healthcare community that being overweight or obese increases our risk of a wide array of medical problems, any of which can hit the fast-forward button on the timetable of death?

## The Slippery Slope of Being Overweight

Exactly what are these problems? Where can being overweight or obese lead? Here are a number of places you don't want to go physically, dangerous destinations along the slippery slope of eating for pleasure and convenience instead of health.

*Coronary artery disease (CAD).* This is the condition produced by the buildup of plaque in the arteries that carry blood to the heart muscles. As heart specialists, we see some form of CAD every day, and virtually all of these patients are overweight or obese. They are heart attacks waiting to happen. CAD patients come in with blockages in their coronary arteries in need of bypass surgery or stents in order to prevent heart attack.

*Stroke.* Stroke results when one of the arteries supplying blood to the brain becomes narrowed or blocked, often by plaque or hardening of the arteries.

*Diabetes.* Approximately 75 percent of all patients with Type II diabetes are also overweight or obese.

*Hypertension.* For the person who is obese, hypertension—high blood pressure—is a given. Being overweight or obese can trigger hypertension.

*Hyperlipidemia and high cholesterol.* The buildup of fats and cholesterol in the bloodstream is directly linked to being overweight and obesity.

*Osteoarthritis.* Degenerative joint disease, or osteoarthritis, develops as the body wears down under excessive weight; and the ankles, knees, and hips begin to deteriorate under the pressure. It is not uncommon to find obese people age fifty or younger coming in for bilateral knee and/or hip replacement, severely limiting mobility or sentencing them to a wheelchair.

*Cancer.* Obesity has been linked to specific types of kidney cancer, colon cancer, and, in women, postmenopausal breast cancer and endometrial cancer.

*Sleep apnea.* Think about the last time you were x-rayed at the dentist. Remember wearing that heavy lead "apron" that protected your vital organs from the x-rays? Did you notice that it impaired your breathing somewhat simply because of the extra weight? That's what sleep apnea does, a breathing disorder characterized by brief interruptions of breathing during sleep. Being overweight or obese is like wearing a lead apron all the time, restricting and interrupting breathing.

*Infertility.* Infertility has been shown to be increased in women who are obese. A condition called polycystic ovarian disease is associated with obesity and infertility. Obesity in men, however, does not seem to affect fertility.

*Gallstones.* Gallstones are clusters of solid material, made mostly from cholesterol, that form in the gallbladder and can cause severe disease as a result of acute inflammation. Carrying extra weight and obesity linked to high levels of cholesterol are definite contributors to gallstones.

*Gout.* Gout is a very painful disease caused by an elevated level of uric acid in the bloodstream. When the level becomes too high, crystals of uric acid form in various joints in the body, causing intense inflammation. Gout has a much higher incidence in patients who are overweight or obese.

## Reversing the Deadly Trend

Here are three health axioms that will, if heeded, dramatically diminish your risk of developing any of these many problems. These axioms are stated by Dr. Walter Willett in his excellent book, *Eat, Drink, and Be Healthy.*[7]

*Next to smoking, your weight is the most important measure of your future health.* Your BMI identifies a safe weight range for your height. You may look at the chart and exclaim, "I haven't been at that weight since I was in high school!" Don't let that number be a tyrant in your life. Total Heart Health is about embracing a lifestyle that will keep you moving toward your weight goals instead of drifting away from a healthy weight range. The apostle Paul spoke about finishing the course laid out for him in the face of many obstacles (see 2 Timothy 4:7). You may never be able to fit into your prom gown again, but every step in that direction, no matter how small, is a positive step toward a healthier, longer life. Stay in the race and finish well.

*Limiting daily calorie intake is the single most important strategy for controlling weight.* Calories supply the energy our bodies need to function. We gain energy by eating, because food contains calories. We expend energy through activity, because everything we do burns calories. The math is very simple. If you take in more calories than you burn, the unused calories are stored as fat and you gain weight. But if you take in fewer calories than you use up, your body burns some of your stored fat for energy and you lose weight.

We call this "energy balance": total daily energy (calories) consumed minus total daily energy expended. If you want to maintain your weight, the numbers on both sides of this equation must be roughly equal—you must burn off about what you take in. But if you want to lose weight, you must burn more energy than you take in.

The recommendations for controlling weight that we present in this book infer that you keep tabs on the number of calories you consume. We're not insisting that you tote a calculator to the meal table at home and to a restaurant when you eat out. Instead, you just need a good working knowledge of the approximate calorie count in what you eat. Calorie-counting booklets are available at your local bookstore.

There's no way around it: weight loss and weight control require your active participation, and buying in to our recommendations means tracking daily calorie intake. You must also know how many daily calories you need to maintain your level of activity.

*A healthy diet, combined with regular exercise and no smoking, can eliminate 80 percent of heart disease and 70 percent of some cancers.* This is a marvelous payoff, isn't it? Give care to diet and exercise, and your odds will soar for a longer, healthier life in which to serve God, help people, and enjoy life. This is an achievable outcome because weight control is a doable activity for any woman. We're going to teach you how to eat foods that are good for you—foods you can get at the local supermarket—and how to avoid the foods that adversely affect your health. And if you know that you need to start losing weight, we have provided a 21-day, low-calorie menu plan with delicious recipes in chapter 21 that you can adopt or adapt to your lifestyle.

Combining healthy calorie intake (energy in) and healthy calorie expenditure (energy out) leads to a healthy life. In the next chapter, we will talk about the energy-out side of the equation.

# Keys to Total Heart Health

## Chapter 8: Are You Eating to Live or Living to Eat?

- God designed the body in such a way that we must *eat to live*, but our culture has bombarded us with the twisted, appealing message that we must *live to eat*.

- If you eat the right kinds of foods in appropriate quantities, you will maximize your opportunities to live a long, productive life.

- When you consistently take in more fuel than you burn, the body must find a place to store the excess, resulting in fat.

- One of the helpful tools for determining how much weight is too much is called body mass index (BMI). A BMI of 25 or greater indicates a person is overweight, 30 or greater indicates obesity, and 40 or greater indicates morbid obesity.

- Being overweight or obese can lead to coronary heart disease, stroke, diabetes, hypertension, hyperlipidemia and high cholesterol, osteoarthritis, cancer, sleep apnea, infertility, gallstones, and gout.

- Three axioms that will diminish your health risk:

  1. Next to smoking, your weight is the most important measure of future health.

  2. Limiting daily calorie intake is the single most important strategy for controlling weight.

  3. A healthy diet, combined with regular exercise and no smoking, can eliminate 80 percent of heart disease and 70 percent of some cancers.

# 9

# Calories: Are They Friend or Foe?

Achieving healthy energy balance
is all about healthy calorie balance.

**Dr. Michael Duncan and Dr. Richard Leachman**

It takes Ellie and Jack twice as long to buy their groceries as most people in the supermarket. Before any box or bag or bottle or jar goes into the shopping cart, it must survive their careful scrutiny. Turning to the "Nutrition Facts" side of the label, they zero in on the top category: calories per serving.

It's kind of a contest between them for each packaged item. Studying a label, Jack reports, "Here's a breakfast cereal with 180 calories per cup."

Down the aisle Ellie responds, "Got you beat. Here's a cereal with 140."

Jack scans four more boxes before announcing, "One thirty."

"One twenty."

"One ten."

The tension mounts as they inspect box after box. Finally Ellie exults, "Ninety calories a serving! Gotcha, Jack."

The cereal goes into the shopping cart, Jack offers Ellie a high-five, and they move on to the next aisle for another contest.

For Ellie and Jack, calories are viewed as a necessary evil. So they are intent on eating the fewest calories possible—and they still feel guilty eating any at all. To be sure, calories can be a harmful enemy to a woman's heart health. But they are not to be feared or banned from your diet. Calories are only your enemy when you let them run wild or when you fail to get the calories your body needs.

## Finding Your Calorie-Need Profile

We need calories to live, so we must eat calories every day. Calories are utilized as energy for everything we do. How much energy is in a calorie? Scientifically speaking, one calorie is the amount of energy needed to raise the temperature of one liter of water by one degree centigrade ($1^{\circ}$ C). On a more practical level, one calorie is the amount of energy expended by a 150-pound woman every minute she is sleeping. A woman at this weight will burn up approximately 480 calories during eight hours of sleep. That's right, you are burning up calories every moment you're alive, even when you are sleeping. What a great way to lose weight! It's just that you're not burning up very many calories during sleep compared to the calories you take in when you're awake.

So the big question is, how much energy—in other words, how many calories—do you need each day to maintain a healthy life? There is no magic number of calories that fits every person. Daily caloric needs are different for each of us depending on height, weight, gender, age, and activity level. So you need to determine what we call your individual calorie-need profile. Your profile takes into account two factors: your basal metabolic rate and the intensity of your weekly physical activity.

### Basal Metabolic Rate

Your basal metabolic rate (BMR) measures the amount of calorie fuel your body requires just to keep you alive with all your organs functioning. Most diets allow more calories for men than for women because they tend to have a higher BMR than women, meaning men burn more calories. Women usually have a higher BMR during pregnancy and lactation because these stages require more energy.

Children and youth have a very high BMR to fuel their growth. That's why most growing, active kids can load up on pizza and burgers and doughnuts and soda without putting on much weight. They are like racecars at burning food fuels. But adults don't need as much calorie power to maintain life. Whenever adults eat like teenagers, we usually end up paying for it with extra pounds. And from midlife on, it seems we don't need to eat much at all to maintain ideal body weight.

Like your BMI, your BMR requires a simple calculation: body weight in kilograms times 24. To determine your weight in kilograms, divide your weight in pounds by 2.2, then multiply your kilogram weight by 24 to arrive at your BMR—the daily number of calories your body requires to maintain life. For example, Ellie's weight of 130 pounds translates to 59 kilograms. Multiplied by 24, her weight in kilograms equates to a BMR of 1,416. So Ellie needs an average of just over 1,400 calories each day just to live.

But the "B" in BMR is *basal*, meaning it is only the starting point. BMR quantifies the needs of a woman who is completely sedentary—no exercise, no activity, just living and breathing, heart beating, kidneys and liver functioning. Unless Ellie is in a coma or is a total invalid, she needs more than 1,400 calories a day. In addition to her BMR, she needs enough calories to adequately fuel all her activities—and so do you.

## Activity Level

The other element for determining your calorie-need profile is your activity level. You must add to your BMR the number of calories you burn for the activity level of your daily life. For example, Ellie leads a very active life. Working forty hours a week for a parcel delivery service, she is on the go all day long—a lot of walking and jogging and a fair bit of lifting. Ellie and Jack also play in a coed volleyball league at the local YMCA. So Ellie is working out, practicing, or playing matches six evenings each week. Her moderate to high activity level requires a lot of calorie fuel, about double that of her BMR. So we multiply Ellie's BMR by 2, pushing her calorie-need profile to near 3,000. This is the average number of calories she needs to live and stay active at her level.

By comparison, let's talk about Anna, a seventy-four-year-old woman who lives in a retirement complex. Anna also weighs 130 pounds, giving her a BMR equal to Ellie's: 1,416. But Anna's activity level is significantly different from Ellie's. On a typical day, Anna rises to eat breakfast, read her Bible and the newspaper, and water her tiny backyard garden. After lunch she lies down on the sofa to watch television and nap. Evening is more of the same—unless it's bingo night in the community room. Anna's low activity level requires significantly fewer calories than that of someone like Ellie, only about a third of her BMR. Multiplying Anna's BMR by about 1.3, her daily calorie-need profile is in the 1,800 range.

Your calorie-need profile likely falls somewhere between that of a retiree like Anna and a dynamo like Ellie. The charts below will help you approximate how many calories you burn in your daily activities. The more strenuous the activity, the more calories you use. Add that number to your BMR and you have your calorie-need profile—a rough idea of the calorie energy your body needs each day.

| Type of Exercise | Calories/hour | Type of Exercise | Calories/hour | Type of Exercise | Calories/hour |
|---|---|---|---|---|---|
| Sleeping | 55 | Dancing, ballroom | 260 | Swimming, active | 500+ |
| Eating | 85 | Walking, 3 mph | 280 | Cross-country ski machine | 500+ |
| Sewing | 85 | Tennis | 350+ | Hiking | 500+ |
| Sitting | 85 | Water aerobics | 400 | Step aerobics | 550+ |
| Standing | 100 | Skating/rollerblading | 420+ | Rowing | 550+ |
| Office work | 140 | Dancing/aerobic | 420+ | Power walking | 600+ |
| Housework, moderate | 160+ | Aerobics | 450+ | Cycling, studio | 650 |
| Golf, with cart | 180 | Bicycling, moderate | 450+ | Skipping with rope | 700+ |
| Golf, without cart | 240 | Jogging, 5 mph | 500 | Running | 700+ |
| Gardening, planting | 250 | Gardening, digging | 500 | | |

## Putting Calories to Work for You

Here's the bottom line to your calorie-need profile: if your profile is roughly equal to the number of calories you take in, your weight will remain about the same week in and week out. You are in what we call energy balance: your energy out is about the same as your energy in. However, if your calorie intake is greater than your profile, you will gain weight because the surplus will be stored as fat. But if you take in fewer calories than your profile, you will lose weight because your body burns off the surplus to compensate for the calorie deficit. Weight loss is as simple as that.

How great a calorie deficit do you need to shed pounds? It might be helpful to know that there are 3,500 calories in one pound of fat. So to lose one pound, you need a calorie deficit of 3,500 calories—meaning your energy out must exceed your energy in by 3,500 calories. Theoretically, if you managed a calorie deficit of 3,500 calories each day, you would lose one pound a day. But we're not in favor of such crash programs—because the "crash" could hurt you more than it helps. We have a more sane and sensible approach in mind.

Here's what we recommend. If your calorie-need profile is somewhere between Ellie's and Anna's—say 2,200 to 2,400 calories—and you want to gradually shed pounds, try a 1,000-calorie-per-day deficit. In other words, subtract 1,000 calories from your calorie-need profile and use that total as a daily goal for calorie intake. At 1,000 calories per day, your weekly deficit will be 7,000 calories. And since there are 3,500 calories in a pound of fat, you could lose about two pounds a week.

Now two pounds in seven days may not seem very glamorous compared to the outrageous claims made by some of the fad weight-loss programs on the market. But it is a realistic, safe, and relatively painless way to take off unwanted pounds. Think about it: at two pounds a week, a severely obese person can lose 104 pounds during the course of a year. Think what you can do in a year! Simply adopt a healthy, balanced weekly menu that fits within your daily target calorie count and watch the pounds and inches slip away.

If your daily calorie-need profile is closer to that of a very active Ellie at 2,500 to 3,000 calories, you may want to try a 1,500-calorie deficit to lose weight faster. But for someone like Anna, whose profile is much lower, a 1,000-calorie deficit may be too harsh. You may want to back off to a 700- to 800-calorie deficit. The pounds will come off more slowly, but as long as you operate in deficit mode, you will lose weight.

## Tips for Weight-Control Success

Losing weight, even a pound or two a month, is a challenge. And keeping the pounds off is an even greater challenge. But a ten-year study called the National Weight Control Registry provides encouragement and hope that you can achieve and maintain your weight-loss goals.[1] More than four thousand people have participated in the study. Here are a few insights gained from the findings.

### Stop Gaining Weight

Most people in America are gaining weight, so if you can neutralize weight gain, you are ahead of the curve and should feel a measure of success.[2] Perhaps an intermediate weight-loss goal for you is to achieve energy balance—eliminating further weight gain. You should feel some satisfaction about staying at the same dress size for a year or more and getting more mileage out of your wardrobe.

## Proceed with Small, Manageable Goals

When you're ready to lose some pounds, studies show that you are more likely to succeed if you take small steps. For example, here is a woman whose body mass index is a very unhealthy 38. She needs to lose at least eighty pounds to reverse the damage her obesity is wreaking in her body. But losing eighty pounds is an extremely daunting goal, like climbing Mount Everest might be to a novice mountain climber. However, losing fifteen to twenty pounds and maintaining that loss is manageable for most people. By reaching a modest goal, this obese woman will be more confident and hopeful about beginning her next campaign to take off another fifteen to twenty pounds.

## Play the Weight-Loss Percentages

Successful weight loss is defined as losing 10 percent of your initial body weight and not regaining it. In other words, it is better to lose ten pounds and keep it off than to lose twenty pounds, gain it back, lose it again, and so on. Using this definition, only 20 percent of the participants in the study were termed "successful" because the others could not keep from regaining the weight loss. There were two main behavioral reasons for this lack of success. First, the study found that these people focused too much on diet and not enough on exercise. Second, they focused on losing the weight but not on keeping it off.

## Diet and Exercise

In the study, there was no dominant motive and no dominant diet and exercise plan for successful weight loss. Some people entered the study to improve health, some to look better, others to feel better, still others to build self-esteem. And the diet plans and exercise regimens employed were all over the map. But there was one clearly common approach to losing weight: 89 percent of those who succeeded did so through diet and exercise. Only 10 percent of the participants succeeded using diet alone, and barely 1 percent lost weight using exercise alone. It's hard to argue with success.

Here are several common factors of diet and exercise for those in the study who succeeded in reaching and maintaining their weight goals:

*Participants averaged 1,300 to 1,500 calories per day consumed.* Compare this to the national average of 3,500 calories consumed per day. This is why most people across the country are gaining weight. The weight-loss menu plan we provide in chapter 21 provides approximately 1,300 calories per day.

*All ate breakfast regularly.* Many people mistakenly believe that skipping breakfast is the way to lose weight. This study suggests otherwise. Eating a nutritious breakfast can help jump-start your metabolism for burning calories all day long.

*Seventy-five percent weighed themselves regularly, either daily or weekly.* We believe consistent weigh-ins—at least weekly—are important. You need to check your weight often to make sure your program is working. If you are not losing weight, there's something wrong with your diet math. Either you're taking in too many calories or you're not burning off enough calories.

*All participated in extensive physical activity.* Women burned an average of 2,500 calories per day through basal metabolic rate and sixty to ninety minutes of moderate to intense exercise. However, in most cases, women in the study weren't on a jogging track or a treadmill or in an aerobics class for sixty to ninety minutes a day. Rather, they counted some of their daily activity as calorie-burning exercise.

For example, many participants in the study wore pedometers—small devices that clip to a belt and count your steps. Women who did a lot of walking during the day counted it as part of their exercise. For example, twelve thousand steps translates into six miles of walking, which burns about six hundred calories. When it comes to cardio exercise, it is preferable to sustain physical activity over a certain time period, like forty minutes of jogging, swimming laps, or an aerobic routine. But for burning calories, all your activities count toward your daily target.

Our Total Heart Health recommendation for every woman is at least thirty minutes of moderate exercise six days per week. Walking is a good example. You can cover about two miles in thirty minutes of brisk walking. At 100 calories a mile, you will burn 200 calories a day, 1,200 calories a week, and 62,400 calories a year. And since one pound of fat equates to 3,500 calories, you could potentially lose about eighteen pounds a year just from eating right and walking two miles a day.

# The Drudgery of the "D Word"

The importance of monitoring calorie intake brings us to the "D word"—*diet*. Most people have tried at least one form of dieting, and most dieters have experienced the frustration of "falling off the wagon" and failing to accomplish their dieting goals. Calories and carbs, protein and portions, fats and fasting—it all gets so confusing. For many women today, *diet* is right up there with other four-letter words we avoid uttering. It seems like weight-control plans are the enemy of a healthy heart instead of a friend.

Why don't diets work? Here are three common answers we hear from women.

### "Diets Are Boring"

Many women complain that the list of foods you can't eat on a diet is much longer than the list of foods you can eat. After a couple of weeks of the "same old, same old" at the dinner table, we lose interest. Life is too short for celery and carrot sticks five times a week.

Our Total Heart Health recommendations include all food groups. We will give you tips on how to navigate through the options to find the foods and portions that are best while steering clear of foods that are clearly detrimental to heart health. The three-week menu of healthy meals we provide in chapter 21 is designed to help you lose weight. Before launching into a new diet plan, especially when it calls for a big change in your calorie intake, talk to your doctor.

### "When I'm on a Diet, I Always Feel Hungry"

The sensation of hunger has a lot to do with blood-sugar level. When your blood sugar takes a dive, your body insists, *I'm starving; let's eat!* We'll talk later about glycemic index and show you how to avoid riding the blood-sugar roller coaster, which so often sends you scurrying to the fridge or the pantry for a snack.

Obviously, hunger also occurs when the stomach shrinks while emptying, and hunger is satisfied when the stomach is full. We will show you the kinds of food that slow down stomach emptying and nutrient absorption so you feel fuller longer.

## "If There Are Cookies or Potato Chips in the House, I Can't Be Trusted"

Exerting self-control in what we eat is not just about food; it's clearly a total heart issue that applies to all of life. The apostle Paul lamented, "I decide to do good, but I don't *really* do it; I decide not to do bad, but then I do it anyway" (Romans 7:19 MSG). Doesn't that sound like the very dilemma we face when trying to choose something healthy from a menu of decadent choices at the local restaurant?

Self-control is an issue of the spiritual heart as much as the physical heart. Paul wrote, "The flesh sets its desire against the Spirit, and the Spirit against the flesh; for these are in opposition to one another, so that you may not do the things that you please" (Galatians 5:17). But then he brings us the good news: "Those who belong to Christ Jesus have crucified the flesh with its passions and desires" (v. 24).

This is why we have teamed with our pastor and his wife to write this book about Total Heart Health. As we have been saying, you can't segment your heart into categories—physical, spiritual, emotional, intellectual. You are a whole person, and each facet of the whole impacts the other facets. The self-discipline you need for establishing healthy habits in your physical life springs from your spiritual life. The chapters provided by Dr. and Mrs. Young are helping you grow in spiritual heart health as we encourage and implement the health of your spiritual heart. The more you build up the spiritual heart muscle, the more it can help you strengthen your physical heart.

Spiritual heart health is also about energy balance: energy in and energy out. In the next chapter, Dr. and Mrs. Young will alert you to the importance of guarding your heart against influences that will rob you of spiritual vitality.

## Chapter 9: Calories: Are They Friend or Foe?

- Daily calorie needs are different for each of us, so you need to determine your individual calorie-need profile, based on your basal metabolic rate (BMR) and the intensity of your weekly physical activity.

- To calculate your BMR, multiply your body weight in kilograms times 24. To determine your weight in kilograms, divide your weight in pounds by 2.2. Then multiply your kilogram weight by 24 to arrive at your BMR—the daily number of calories your body requires to maintain life.

- To find your activity level, add to your BMR the number of calories you burn for your daily activity level. A woman physically active throughout the day might require calorie fuel double that of her BMR. So she would multiply her BMR by two to determine the average number of calories she needs to live and stay active at that level.

- If your calorie-need profile is roughly equal to the number of calories you take in, your weight will remain about the same. If your calorie intake is greater than your profile, the surplus will be stored as fat. If you take in fewer calories than your profile, you will lose weight.

- You're more likely to succeed in losing pounds if you take small steps in a program combining good diet and at least thirty minutes of exercise daily.

# 10
# Four Health Trends
# That Can Hurt Your Heart

Just because "everybody's doing it"
doesn't mean it's right for you.

**Dr. Michael Duncan and Dr. Richard Leachman**

If you're anything like our wives, you're not wearing the same style clothes you wore five years ago—or perhaps even two years ago. Clothing fashions seem to change constantly. Skirts get longer, then shorter, then longer again. Pastels are in for a while, then out, then in again. The same kind of evolution occurs with hairstyles, furniture, house décor, vehicles, and many other facets of our daily lives. There's nothing wrong with constantly changing fashions, though it can be expensive trying to keep up with all the trends.

There are also trends when it comes to physical health. During the past several decades, there has been a fair amount of evolution in our country's approach to diet and exercise. Medical authorities, including some of the national medical societies, continue to update health recommendations to reflect concerns about health issues, especially coronary artery disease and heart disease in general, the number one killer in the United States. And along with these recommendations come many popular trends for how we should take care of our bodies.

Changing your wardrobe to keep up with current fashion isn't likely to affect your physical health. Nor will it be a health issue when you change the cut or color of your hair or redecorate your bedroom with the latest fabrics and furnishings. However, trying to keep up with some of the popular trends for diet and exercise *can* be harmful to your health. Here are four such trends that should be approached with caution because of the possible negative impact on your heart health.

## Trend 1: Forgo All Fats

As it became clear that abnormal cholesterol levels in the bloodstream are a risk factor in developing heart disease, the American Heart Association and other national health authorities recommended that patients should follow a diet low in fat—particularly saturated fat—and cholesterol. Most doctors around the country passed these recommendations along to their patients and to the general public. As a result, a popular health trend has gained wide acceptance: *all fats are bad, so we should exclude fat from our diet.*

How has this trend taken hold in our culture? An entire food industry has grown up around this trend. You can see it every time you go into the super-market. Notice how many food products on the shelf are labeled "fat-free," "nonfat," "low-fat," "reduced fat," "less fat," "lite," and so on. You can also see it every time you go out to eat. Many restaurants today highlight menu items that are low in fat and considered healthier for the heart. Be honest now: when you go out for lunch, don't you at least consider the option of ordering a big salad—with fat-free dressing—instead of a burger and fries?

As doctors, we have a couple of problems with the trend to forgo all fats. First, we disagree with the assumption that all fats are bad, because this assumption is false. Dietary fat in proper amounts is essential for normal body health because fat is a necessary component of cell membranes in the body. Fat regulates and facilitates the production, distribution, and function of good cholesterol. It is involved in the absorption and distribution of fat-soluble vita-mins including D, E, A, and K. Fat is important in the insulation of nerves and aids in nerve conduction. Fat is present to a large degree in the brain and is part of normal brain function.

Fat—in the form of adipose tissue—is the major fuel storage component of our bodies. We all need a certain amount of adipose tissue to insulate the body against extreme temperatures, to cushion the vital organs, and to store potential energy. Consequently, not all fats are bad. In fact, being swept along by this trend to avoid all fatty foods like the plague may even negatively affect your health.

Another problem we see with this trend is the built-in temptation to excess. For example, you bring home from the market reduced-fat ice cream or low-fat sandwich spread or "lite" salad dressing. Since these products are "healthier," you tend to serve larger portions of them. You think, *It's not as bad for me, so I can eat more of it.* By upping our portion sizes in this way, we not only cancel out some of the benefits of lowering fat consumption, but we also tend to eat more overall calories.

We will talk about the proper balance of fats in the diet when we get to chapter 13, which covers the three primary dietary fuels: fats, carbohydrates, and protein.

## Trend 2: Cancel Out Carbs

As the trend to avoid fats grew, where did people turn to fill up the empty space on their dinner plates? To carbohydrates. They cut back on fatty red meats and piled on more "harmless" potatoes and breads, prompting the health community to issue new warnings about eating carbs in relatively unlimited quantities. This warning has given rise to a carb-conscious trend, carving out another new niche in the food industry: carb-free and low-carb foods. We adopted the mind-set that carbohydrates are as bad for us as fats, so we'd better cancel them out of our diet too.

The anti-carb trend opened the door for numerous low-carbohydrate diets, some of which are very popular—the Atkins Diet and the Sugar Busters Diet, among others. These dietary plans correctly point out that some types of carbohydrates, particularly simple carbohydrates, can be metabolized into the bloodstream quite rapidly, resulting in wide swings in blood sugar. The low-carb or carb-free diets are aimed at controlling high spikes in blood sugar that tend to encourage overeating and weight gain.

The biology of rapidly metabolized simple carbohydrates is reflected in what is called the *glycemic index*. This index shows how quickly the carbohydrates in certain foods are broken down into glucose and enter the bloodstream to elevate blood sugar. Foods with a high glycemic index cause a rapid rise in blood sugar, and foods with a low glycemic index prompt a slower rise in blood sugar. The overall desired response is for blood sugar to rise gradually and fall gradually. This response is achieved by consuming fewer foods known to have a high glycemic index.

The carbohydrates that most need to be controlled are known as simple carbohydrates, also called simple sugars. Simple carbs are those that are more easily broken down during digestion. Complex carbohydrates take longer to break down, so the rise in blood sugar is more gradual. Here's a good example of the two. When you drink a glass of apple juice (simple carbohydrate), it will hit your system fast and spike your blood sugar to a high level very quickly. But if you eat an apple (complex carbohydrate), it takes your system longer to digest it, resulting in a much more gradual rise in blood sugar.

Refined foods such as white breads, pastries, packaged cookies, and cakes have a high glycemic index. This is because the refining process eliminates the bran and germ components from the wheat kernel, leaving only the endosperm and the white flour, which essentially jump-start the digestive process. Wheat germ has B complex vitamins, vitamin E, and trace minerals. Wheat bran is a great source of fiber, and both elements have high quantities of B vitamins and other micronutrients. The endosperm has much less nutritive value and is a simple carbohydrate quickly metabolized to produce high blood sugar. This is why whole-grain products are much better for you than refined products. The following chart provides some sampling of foods categorized from very low to very high on the glycemic index.

Why is this important? Let's say you gulp down a jelly sandwich on white bread, a twelve-ounce can of sugary soda, and a candy bar for lunch—a meal that is loaded with simple sugars. Your blood sugar will soon skyrocket, prompting your pancreas to secrete insulin into the bloodstream to capture this sugar and use it for energy. As the blood sugar continues to surge, the insulin goes into high gear and drives the blood sugar way down to keep it under control. When blood sugar plummets, the body begins to nag at you, "I am hungry." That's why you hustle off to the pantry or the snack wagon when it pulls up outside your workplace. And if you choose high-glycemic snacks, you are setting yourself up for being very hungry at dinnertime. You end up eating too much, and the added weight taxes your heart.

One of the bad results of this vicious cycle is the potential for insulin resistance. For someone who is overweight, the body does not respond to insulin in the normal way. As a result, blood sugar in the system can remain high for long periods, causing the pancreas to produce more insulin. This can result in Type II diabetes, and you do not want to go there.

## Glycemic Index of Certain Foods

| Food | | Food | | Food | |
|---|---|---|---|---|---|
| Artificial sweeteners | >5 | Orange juice | 52 | Potato, mashed | 70 |
| Diet soda, without caffeine | 0 | Bananas | 54 | Tortilla, corn | 70 |
| Grapefruit | 25 | Sweet potato | 54 | Bagel, white | 72 |
| Whole milk | 27 | Rice, brown | 55 | Watermelon | 72 |
| Butter beans | 31 | Sweet corn | 55 | Cheerios | 74 |
| Lima beans | 32 | Honey | 58 | Graham crackers | 74 |
| Skim milk | 32 | Rice, white | 58 | Potato, French fries | 75 |
| Apples | 38 | Cheese pizza | 60 | Doughnuts, plain | 76 |
| Tomato soup | 38 | Hamburger bun | 61 | Vanilla wafers | 77 |
| Pinto beans | 39 | Ice cream | 61 | White bread | 78 |
| Snickers bar | 40 | Oatmeal, quick | 61 | Pretzels | 81 |
| Spaghetti, white | 41 | Black bean soup | 64 | Rice Krispies | 82 |
| Oranges | 44 | Chocolate chip cookies | 64 | Cornflakes | 83 |
| Linguini | 46 | Macaroni & cheese | 64 | Potato, baked | 85 |
| Grapefruit juice | 48 | Raisins | 64 | Rice, white, instant | 90 |
| Carrots | 49 | Sucrose (table sugar) | 64 | Gatorade | 95 |
| Oatmeal, regular | 49 | Soft drinks | 68 | Glucose | 100 |

Not all carbohydrates are good. There may be times when you crave a sugar high, but ideally, you should focus on carbs with a low glycemic index. But contrary to what many people think, not all carbohydrates are bad. There are certain complex carbohydrates with a low glycemic index that provide valuable nutritional elements and should not be eliminated from the diet. Examples of these would include fruits, vegetables, and whole-grain products. So while some of the principles of the low-carb diets are valid, we believe trying to cancel all carbs out of your diet leads to an unbalanced diet and is unwise. We will share more about carbs in chapter 13.

## Trend 3: Eat More, Move Less

This trend didn't have its origin in the health community; it is a reflection of American culture and consumerism. It's the widespread trend to eat more than we need and exercise less than we should. This trend is like a double-barreled shotgun aimed right at your heart. It is the primary reason that we are experiencing an epidemic of overweight and obese people in this country.

You can see signs of the "eat more" side of this trend wherever food is found. Think about the all-you-can-eat specials offered at many restaurants and the popularity of buffet-style restaurants. In these situations, diners almost feel obligated to go back for seconds and thirds just to get their money's worth. Think about fast-food places where "extra-large" or "super-sized" combos cost only parking-meter change more than regular-sized ones. These tantalizing offers appeal to our sense of value: getting more for less.

In every aisle of the supermarket you are tempted by the "value" of buying sizes of packaged foods larger than what you really need or taking advantage of "buy one, get one free" specials. Almost every family these days can join one of the popular warehouse chains where you can buy foods—including those you should eat only in moderation—in bulk quantities at even greater savings. The end result of bargain shopping is a full pantry that tempts many families to prepare and serve larger quantities of food at the dinner table.

We are also influenced to eat more than we should through the medium of advertising. For example, in a TV commercial, dinner plates are piled high with pasta. Why? Because if you take the hint and pile your plate just as high, the pasta company will make more money. When we buy more, cook more, serve more, and eat more as advertising often encourages, it means more profit for everyone in the "food chain"—except for the consumer, who must deal with the added calories and pounds.

There's nothing wrong with buying food in volume quantities as long as you still serve it and eat it in healthy portions. Unfortunately, a lot of people are lacking in this discipline. The United States Department of Agriculture (USDA) notes that the average American consumes around 3,500 calories per day, which is roughly twice as much as the normal adult needs to maintain ideal body weight. This is a trend that can kill you. *How much* you eat is at least as important as *what* you eat. In part 3, we will show you how to eat the right foods in the right quantities.

Eating more is especially harmful when it is coupled with the other facet of this trend: moving less. American culture during the past several decades is trending away from a physically active lifestyle to one that is much more sedentary. Thanks to technology, many of us have machines to do the "labor" that a previous generation had to perform by the sweat of their brow. So we move less on the job, with many of us sitting stationary a good portion of the workday. We take the escalator or elevator instead of climbing the stairs. We drive or take the bus when we could walk.

Almost everybody knows it's good to participate in moderate regular exercise as a way to burn up some of the excess calories that most of us consume. Regular exercise provides many other benefits, including stress relief, cardiovascular health, muscle tone, and flexibility. But many of us have trouble carving out time for exercise in our busy lives and maintaining an exercise program that is boring or difficult. In chapter 17, we will share with you exercise options that will help you put together a program that is right for you—and fun!

The damaging "eat more, move less" trend must be reversed. Almost all of us would do well to eat less—as well as smarter—and move more through regular, purposeful exercise.

## Trend 4: Eat on the Run

Your son has a dentist appointment right after school, then he goes straight to soccer practice at five o'clock. You drop him off at the field, hurry to pick up your daughter from cheerleading practice, and shuttle her to Brittany's house for pizza with other ninth-grade student council leaders. Picking up Jason from soccer, you only have a half-hour before you must leave for a parents' meeting at the school. What do you do for dinner tonight? Thank goodness for drive-through windows at places like McDonald's, Wendy's, Taco Bell, Pizza Hut, and KFC.

This scenario reflects another societal trend that can work against heart health. Life for so many of us runs at such a fast pace that meal preparation is more an issue of convenience than nutrition. The combination of our jobs, our other activities, the kids' activities, church activities, classes, sports, and so on leaves little time and energy for planning and preparing nutritious meals. So it is often simpler and easier to stop at a fast-food place en route or to pick up a precooked meal on the fly.

The problem is that convenient eating is not always nutritious eating. The calorie count for a meal in a box or a bag is sometimes off the charts, way more than an adult or a child needs to maintain ideal body weight. The bread products you get are usually refined instead of whole grain. The meats are often high in fat and/or cooked in fat. Fruits and vegetables are seldom an option for these meals. And a fast-food lunch or dinner just doesn't seem to be complete without French fries. To top it off, you can super-size your order or get a combo meal for only a few cents more.

Don't get us wrong; we're not campaigning to close down fast-food restaurants. As you know, many of these establishments offer relatively healthy options, such as salads, low-calorie sub sandwiches, whole-grain breads, and grilled meats. And in reality, an occasional fast-food combo meal or slice of pepperoni pizza dripping with cheese won't kill you. But whenever you need a quick lunch or dinner on the run for yourself and your family, we recommend that you select healthy meals in sensible portions. And we encourage you to balance your occasional fast-food experiences with nutritious, well-balanced, calorie-conscious meals you can prepare at home.

Our approach to heart health in this book is not a new fad diet and exercise plan you will grow tired of in three months. Total Heart Health is an ongoing lifestyle that will help you rise above the temptations that come with the popular trends in food and exercise. Since our approach to health does not eliminate any food groups, you will enjoy a wide variety of options for diet and exercise that won't leave you feeling restricted or punished as so many plans do.

Not only is your physical health at risk due to misconceptions about food and exercise, but your spiritual health may be endangered by myths that can erode your faith and weaken your spiritual heart. Dr. and Mrs. Young will address this vital topic in the next chapter.

# Keys to Total Heart Health

## Chapter 10: Four Health Trends
## That Can Hurt Your Heart

- During the past several decades, there has been a fair amount of evolution in our country's approach to diet and exercise.

- Trying to keep up with some of the popular trends for diet and exercise can be harmful to your health.

- *Trend 1: Forgo All Fats.* Dietary fat in proper amounts is essential for normal body health. When we eat more "fat-free" foods, we tend to eat more overall calories.

- *Trend 2: Cancel Out Carbs.* Not all carbohydrates are bad. Certain complex carbohydrates, such as fruits, vegetables, and whole-grain products, provide valuable nutritional elements and should not be eliminated from the diet.

- *Trend 3: Eat More, Move Less.* The widespread trend to eat more and exercise less is the primary reason that we are experiencing an epidemic of overweight and obese people in this country.

- *Trend 4: Eat on the Run.* Whenever you need a quick meal on the run, select healthy meals in sensible portions. And balance your occasional fast-food experiences with nutritious, well-balanced, calorie-conscious meals you can prepare at home.

- The Total Heart Health plan is not a new fad diet and exercise plan; it's an ongoing lifestyle that will help you rise above the temptations that come with the popular trends in food and exercise.

# 11
# Five Fears That Will Erode Your Faith

If you can trust God for anything,
why can't you trust Him for everything?

**Ed and Jo Beth Young**

If it is your purpose and practice to maintain a strong spiritual heart through your faith in God, you have a great advantage for a healthy life. Consider some of the scientific findings:

- Research focusing on psychotherapy found that "religious patients who received treatment with religious content had better outcomes than patients, religious or not, with whom religious content was omitted."[1]

- The *American Journal of Psychiatry* reported that elderly people with "strong religious faith" got over depression more quickly than those without faith in God.[2]

- Dr. Harold G. Koenig of Duke University found that heart-surgery patients at Dartmouth Medical Center with strong faith had a mortality rate one-third lower than those who did not.[3]

- Researchers at the University of California, Berkeley, discovered that "those who go to church once a week or more have 25–35 percent lower mortality rates from all causes than nonchurchgoers."[4]

- There was even evidence that "those people who are attending church might actually have stronger immune systems."[5]

One reason belief in God is good for heart health is that a believing heart rests. Faith helps us put the whole weight of our stresses on the strong shoulders of Him in whom we trust. We don't trust in "faith"; we trust in God. Consequently, the heart of faith is filled with hope, which contributes to a healthy outlook. Scientists studying elderly people with faith who got over depression more quickly speculated that "religious faith may provide such persons with a sense of hope that things will turn out all right regardless of their problems and, thus, foster greater motivation to achieve emotional recovery."[6]

No wonder your soul's enemy is always trying to mug you and heist your faith! When your faith wanes, so does your physical, emotional, and spiritual health. How does he attack your faith? With fear. Satan is the ultimate terrorist, working to scare you into a corner where your influence for Christ in your world is neutralized.

We want to share with you five fears the enemy uses to rob a woman of health-giving faith. If you fail to take a stand against the enemy's terrorism in your life, you will miss out on the Total Heart Health benefits God provides through a life of faith.

## Fear 1: Afraid to Trust God for Your Children

How do you think Mary, the mother of Jesus, felt the first day Joseph invited their young son to help him in the carpenter shop? I can't imagine Mary wringing her hands with worry and saying something like, "Be careful, Jesus, because there are a lot of sharp tools in there; you could cut off a finger or hand." Or can you hear her saying to Joseph, "No way is my son going to work in such a dangerous trade. I'm sending him to scribe school so he won't get hurt"?

We get a telling glimpse of Mary's concern for her boy in the incident of Jesus's visit to the temple as a twelve-year-old, as recorded in Luke 2:41–52. Upon discovering that Jesus was missing from their caravan of friends and relatives who were returning to Nazareth from Jerusalem, Joseph and Mary hurried back to Jerusalem in panic. Finding Jesus in the temple, Mary said, "Your father and I have been anxiously looking for You" (v. 48). "Anxiously" here speaks of great inner torment, anguish, and distress. Mary was beside herself with concern. Probably no one would have blamed her if she had said something like, "That's it, Jesus; you are never leaving my sight again."

As a mother, I (Jo Beth) can understand how Mary must have felt, and if you're a mother, you can too. For example, how did you feel the day you put your child on a school bus for the first time, or the day he or she wasn't on the bus when it arrived home? What was your reaction when your teenage son said, "Mom, I want to go out for football," or your teenage daughter exulted, "Our youth group is going on a mission trip to the Middle East!" or your college-bound child announced, "I've decided to enlist in the military"?

"That's wonderful," you might have said, trying to cover up your worry with a fake smile while asking God to forgive you for lying.

Obsessive fear of what could happen to your children erodes your trust in God, and you tend to "overmother." You lose faith in God's capacity and willingness to take care of your kids, so you forbid them from doing anything you can't be there to supervise directly. This can smother your children, stunt their development, and make them pull away from you. And overprotective mothering will sap you of mental, emotional, and physical energy. You were not designed to hover over your children twenty-four hours of every day.

Jesus said, "Are not two sparrows sold for a cent? And yet not one of them will fall to the ground apart from your Father. But the very hairs of your head are all numbered. So do not fear; you are more valuable than many sparrows" (Matthew 10:29–31).

You and your children are never outside the Father's care, even when He permits one of them to "fall." Balanced mothering means committing your children to God's care, preparing them for life as best you can without smothering them, and then trusting in the Father's care without fear.

## Fear 2: Afraid to Trust God for Your Finances

Phyllis has been downsized in a job where she was already struggling to make ends meet. She spends many sleepless nights worrying about how she's going to make it with very few financial corners left to cut.

Marie was abruptly widowed four months ago. She is terrified at trying to support herself as an elderly homemaker no one will employ.

Belinda's husband lost his job, and she is panic-stricken at the thought of losing their home.

All these women have heard wonderful sermons about faith, but the immediate threat of financial need looms like a menacing giant in their paths. Their faith in the God of great provision has been undermined by a fear that He cannot or will not meet their current crisis.

Millennia ago a widow lived in a place called Zarephath. In 1 Kings 17, God told the prophet Elijah to go minister in the region, adding that He had "commanded a widow there to provide for you" (v. 9). On arrival, Elijah asked the woman for water and a chunk of bread. The widow replied that she had "only a handful of flour in the bowl and a little oil in the jar" (v. 12). She claimed to be on the brink of starvation.

But Elijah gave the woman a new perspective on her need and God's provision. He asked her to bake him a little bread cake, promising, "For thus says the LORD God of Israel, 'The bowl of flour shall not be exhausted, nor shall the jar of oil be empty, until the day that the LORD sends rain on the face of the earth'" (v. 14).

Great fear of deprivation caused the woman to see nothing but her desperate condition. She assumed God was locked away in the temple with no thought for her crisis. She labored under the delusion that hope for survival rested on her shoulders alone. But God fulfilled His promise. "The bowl of flour was not exhausted nor did the jar of oil become empty, according to the word of the LORD which He spoke through Elijah" (v. 16).

You may not be as destitute as this Old Testament woman was or as needy as Phyllis, Marie, and Belinda mentioned above. But perhaps you have known the panic of a financial squeeze. Unable to see how God will provide, you take on more work than you can handle at the exclusion of everything else. God's plan for your life always includes His provision. The key to your peace and health is getting your focus off the crisis and onto Christ.

Jesus taught, "Do not worry then, saying, 'What will we eat?' or 'What will we drink?' or 'What will we wear for clothing?' For . . . your heavenly Father knows that you need all these things. But seek first His kingdom and His righteousness, and all these things will be added to you" (Matthew 6:31–33).

God was up to something in the midst of the widow's crisis; and if you have put your trust in God, He's at work in the midst of your pressing need as well. Take time to focus on God, ask Him what He's doing in your life, and listen for how you should respond. Watch for His hand, trust Him in the absence of things, and celebrate His coming provision.

## Fear 3: Afraid to Trust God for Your Intimacy Needs

Many women today experience a painful gap between their need for emotional intimacy and the reality of that intimacy in their relationships. The Bible says, "Friends love through all kinds of weather, and families stick together in all kinds of trouble" (Proverbs 17:17 MSG). But friendships and family relationships don't always live up to this standard, and we struggle with the emptiness.

This is true in many marriages. Some husbands are either unable or unwilling to fully meet their wives' needs for closeness and care. Marriage and family counselor Willard Harley found direct evidence of this need gap. "Whenever I asked couples to list their desires according to their priority," said Harley, "men would list them one way and women the opposite way." The five emotional needs "listed as most important by men were usually the least five important for women, and vice-versa."[7]

The members of a loving relationship of any kind, including marriage, should flow together as a single unit, aware of and meeting each other's needs. When a rift occurs between friends or family members because of unmet emotional needs, fear creeps in to suggest that God cannot be trusted to change those who are emotionally closed. For example, many women whose husbands are emotionally aloof tend to respond by withdrawing from them physically, which only widens the gap and leaves husbands vulnerable to sexual temptation.

Husbands are to live with their wives with understanding (see 1 Peter 3:7). Ideally, your husband understands your need for friendship, conversation, listening, and caring. But since there are no perfect husbands—or wives—the only way to live in peace, joy, and emotional health is to trust God to fill the need gap in your life where your husband lacks understanding or follow-through.

In order to replace fear with faith in your close relationships, cultivate intimacy with God, who knows your deepest emotional needs and cares about you. Receive with gladness all that your friends and family members are able to give you in emotional support and intimacy. Trust God as the source of all your emotional intimacy needs. Faith is the bridge that spans the chasm between you and your loved ones no matter how wide it may be. Trusting God in this way, you also may want to seek professional counseling to help you deal with your relational difficulties.

## Fear 4: Afraid to Trust God Because of the Way He Made You

"Most women 'hate their bodies,'" heralded a headline from the British Broadcasting Company.[8] In an AOL survey of forty-five thousand women, six of ten said "they could not stand the way they look," reported the BBC. The proliferation and popularity of personal makeover television programs seem to echo this finding.

Physical beauty is so highly cherished and sought after in society that many women live in fear of not being accepted because of how they look. The woman who hates her body finds it difficult to maintain a loving relationship with God. After all, she reasons, God made her this way; it is His fault. She fears that the God who made her too fat or too skinny or too short or too tall cannot be trusted with anything else important in her life.

If you struggle in your relationship with God and others because you don't like your appearance, you must grasp two vital truths. First, accept the reality of what we will call God's "sovereign artistry." Paul describes it in Romans 9:20–21 like this: "Clay doesn't talk back to the fingers that mold it, saying, 'Why did you shape me like this?' Isn't it obvious that a potter has a perfect right to shape one lump of clay into a vase for holding flowers and another into a pot for cooking beans?" (MSG).

A potter understands the unique purpose to be achieved in every lump of clay. Sometimes the potter will craft an elegant vase to hold flowers. Sometimes she will form earthenware pots and bowls for everyday use. Paul cannot imagine a lump of clay challenging the potter's design and purpose. It is equally ludicrous for us to withdraw from God because of how He made us, or to blame Him for traits we brought on ourselves. We are fashioned for God's purpose, and even if we don't understand it, we must trust that He knows what He's doing.

There is certainly nothing wrong with accentuating your appearance with fashionable clothes, jewelry, hairstyle, and makeup. But your temporal appearance is not as important as your eternal purpose to glorify God with your body and direct others to Him. You will be continually anxious and frustrated while being preoccupied with how you look when God is more concerned with who you are.

In the summer of 1997, England's glamorous Princess Diana was killed in a car crash in Paris. She was only thirty-six. Five days later, on the day of Diana's funeral, another woman of world renown died of heart failure in Calcutta at age eighty-seven. Mother Teresa didn't even receive her calling as a nun until Diana's age at her death: thirty-six. Mother Teresa devoted the rest of her life to the service of Christ by ministering to the world's poorest of the poor.

Which of these two "vessels of clay" was more elegant in appearance? Obviously, it was Diana, a vision of wealth, fashion, and stately beauty. In contrast, Mother Teresa was short, bent, wrinkled, and swathed in a peasant's sari. But did Mother Teresa's common appearance and simple lifestyle disqualify her from accomplishing God's purposes? Absolutely not. Mother Teresa will be remembered as one whose selfless service to Christ and others touched countless numbers of the impoverished, the diseased, and the neglected.

Keep God's purpose for you at the center of your focus, and your preoccupation with your body will be displaced!

Another important principle to grasp is that your acceptance by God is not at all based on your appearance. Paul writes in Ephesians 1:6 that through Christ, God has made us "accepted in the beloved" (KJV). Jesus Christ was the object of His Father's full and complete favor. If you are in Christ, God receives you with the highest honor and greatest favor because of His Son! And it has nothing at all to do with your physical appearance.

A woman's self-perception is often formed by how she perceives she is viewed and accepted by her father, especially during adolescence. Grasp the fact your heavenly Father looks upon you just as you are and smiles at your loveliness. In God's eyes, you have supreme beauty because He made you and His Son fills you. In the end, His acceptance is all that matters.

## Fear 5: Afraid to Trust God to Find a Husband for You

Many single women would like to be married. But when there are no eligible prospects on the horizon, some do whatever they can to attract a man, often winding up in a painful marriage or going through a quick divorce. Why do they force the issue? Fear. They are afraid of being condemned to a lonely, single life or afraid that God's choice for them—whether it be a single life or a potential mate—will not fulfill their hopes and dreams.

When it comes to finding a husband, just as in every other area of life, you must trust in God rather than your own passions, preferences, and plans. Faith in God and His design for love and marriage in your life leads to health; trying to write your own romantic script can be disastrous!

Jesus Christ is your spiritual husband, whether or not you are ever married to a man. And He desires your foremost devotion and allegiance. The apostle Paul writes to the church at Corinth, "I am jealous for you with a godly jealousy; for I betrothed you to one husband, so that to Christ I might present you as a pure virgin." Echoing Christ's love and desire for His bride, the apostle fears the Corinthian believers will be easily led away "from the simplicity and purity of devotion to Christ" (2 Corinthians 11:2–3). Give God your unbridled devotion and let Him fill your longing for a husband.

Here are some suggestions for walking in faith instead of fear regarding your marital future:

- Tell God up-front, "I want only what You want for me, and I am willing to remain single if that is Your plan for me."

- Ask God, "If You want me to be married, direct me to the right man in Your perfect timing."

- Ask God for the grace and gift of singleness and celibacy until the right man comes along at the right time.

- Don't sit around idly waiting for the right man; get on with your life! Having committed yourself and your plans to Christ's lordship, live the full, productive life God has for you right now.

Put your faith in God. Faith provides the rest and hope you desire only when it is placed in the One who is able to give you rest and hope! The power of faith is in the object of our faith: God Himself. The gospel has transforming power "to everyone who believes" (Romans 1:16).

Belief is not a feeling; it is an act of reason and will. It is a choice you make. By God's design and declaration, "the righteous man shall live by faith" (Romans 1:17). If your sins are forgiven and you are gradually being transformed into Christ's image, you are not merely eking out a life of mere survival. You can thrive through the energy of your trust in God.

Biblically grounded, God-directed faith is vital for the well-being of your total heart. Don't let fear stifle that health-giving trust in God!

# Keys to Total Heart Health

## Chapter 11: Five Fears That Will Erode Your Faith

- Faith is vital for heart health because the believing heart rests. Your soul's enemy tries to steal your faith with fear.

- *Fear 1: Afraid to Trust God for Your Children.* Commit your children to God's care, prepare them for life as best you can without smothering them, and then trust in the Father's care without fear.

- *Fear 2: Afraid to Trust God for Your Finances.* If you are in a financial squeeze and are unable to see how God will provide, the key to your peace and health is getting your focus off the crisis and onto Christ.

- *Fear 3: Afraid to Trust God for Your Intimacy Needs.* To replace fear with faith, cultivate intimacy with God and receive emotional support and intimacy from your family and friends.

- *Fear 4: Afraid to Trust God Because of the Way He Made You.* The woman who hates her body finds it hard to have a healthy relationship with God—her Maker. To overcome this, accept God's "sovereign artistry" and remember that your acceptance by God is not based on your appearance.

- *Fear 5: Afraid to Trust God to Find a Husband for You.* When it comes to finding a husband, trust in God rather than your own passions, preferences, and plans. Faith in God and His design for love and marriage leads to health; trying to write your own romantic script can be disastrous!

# 12
# Unblocking the Flow
# to Your Spiritual Heart

Five areas where you may be
in need of "spiritual angioplasty."

**Ed and Jo Beth Young**

Jeanette has a heart problem. When she went to the clinic because she felt crummy all over, her doctor discovered a serious blockage in one of her coronary arteries. It's a potentially life-threatening situation, so Jeanette has been referred to a heart specialist and is scheduled for angioplasty to remove the obstruction.

Rosa has a heart problem. She recently stumbled onto a series of e-mails on her husband's laptop computer—very suggestive e-mails from a woman. Shocked at what she read, Rosa confronted Raul, and he confessed to an extramarital affair with the woman, one of his clients. Deeply hurt, Rosa cried for days. She has an appointment with their pastor, but right now she doesn't think she can stay with Raul. Rosa feels that all her love for her husband has drained out through the huge tear in her heart.

Deedee has a heart problem. For months now, God has seemed distant, invisible, silent. Deedee's long hours at work have pushed Bible reading and prayer to the fringes of her daily life. And the only time she has for Reginald, the new man in her life, is Sunday, so Deedee hasn't been to church in weeks. Her heart feels so dry, so empty. Job stresses are mounting, and her after-work drink with the girls in the office has escalated to two or three drinks. Deedee knows she needs God in her life, but she's afraid she will never find Him again.

Many folks talk about heart problems. Some, like Jeanette, are referring to the physical heart—valves not functioning properly, clogged arteries, arrhythmia. People like Rosa are talking about pain in the emotional heart, describing wounds resulting from discord in a friendship, romance, or family relationship. But the most serious heart problems occur in the spiritual heart, because the spiritual heart is at the core of our being.

This is what Jesus was communicating when He said, "Do you not understand that everything that goes into the mouth passes into the stomach, and is eliminated? But the things that proceed out of the mouth come from the heart, and those defile the man. For out of the heart come evil thoughts, murders, adulteries, fornication, thefts, false witness, slanders. These are the things which defile the man" (Matthew 15:17–20). Blockages in the spiritual heart are serious. Though all the women mentioned above are in pain and in need of heart healing, Deedee is at greatest risk because of the growing darkness in her spiritual heart.

## Searching Out the Source of Heart Blockage

One morning, a friend of ours noticed a foul smell in his house. He searched every room but could not find the source. Day after day the odor intensified, and he became desperate to find the problem. At last he found the source. A doorknob had punched a little round hole in one of the bedroom walls. Apparently a small bird had flown into the house and found its way inside the bedroom wall through that hole. The bird became trapped and died. Our friend was so desperate to remove the stench of death from his house that he was willing to tear out the drywall.

In a similar way, when there is blockage in the spiritual heart, we don't feel right or live right. It's like a foul odor we can't identify. We must do whatever is necessary to find the source and get rid of it, or things will only get worse. This must have been David's determination when he prayed, "Investigate my life, O God, find out everything about me; cross-examine and test me, get a clear picture of what I'm about; see for yourself whether I've done anything wrong—then guide me on the road to eternal life" (Psalm 139:23–24 MSG).

David understood that the corruption in his life came from his heart. From that sick center, infirmity spread over his whole being like the reek of death that seeped through our friend's house. As Deedee discovered, a blockage in the spiritual heart can shut down the flow of spiritual energy and passion for the Lord. David recognized that only God can get to the source of a clogged heart. Only He has the power to rip out the deadness of sin concealed in the hidden depths of our hearts.

How do these debilitating blockages form? Just as plaque builds up in the coronary arteries to block the flow of blood to the physical heart, so our spiritual hearts are blocked when foreign matter enters to compromise their purity. Second Kings 17:33 says that God's people "feared the LORD" but "served their own gods." When the allegiance we owe to God is diverted to other things—a career, a hobby, an addiction—the health of our spiritual hearts is compromised. A divided, compromised heart is weak because the flow of the Spirit's energy to our lives is blocked.

Deedee is floundering spiritually because she has allowed her own interests, priorities, and activities to block God's total access to her heart. She needs "spiritual angioplasty." Like David, she needs a clean heart and a renewed spirit.

Perhaps you see yourself in Deedee's shoes. You may feel distant from God and disconnected from what you know He wants you to be and to do. In this state, it's so easy to beat yourself up mentally, thinking you're no good to God and worthy only of His anger and punishment. Maybe you've been attending this pity party for some time, hoping that the guilt and shame you feel will somehow fix what's wrong.

But by now you may have discovered that condemning yourself this way brings no relief. That's because it was never intended to. Jesus said in Matthew 5:8, "You're blessed when you get your inside world—your mind and heart—put right. Then you can see God in the outside world" (MSG). The opposite of a blocked heart is a pure heart. God is not out to condemn you for having a clogged heart; He wants to make you pure in heart by removing whatever is blocking your fellowship with Him. You will never fully understand and enjoy the blessing and assurance of God unless you allow Him to purify your heart.

## Releasing the Flow in the Spiritual Heart

What do these debilitating spiritual blockages look like? I (Jo Beth) want to talk about five ways the spiritual heart can be blocked and how to return to a pure heart in each case.

## The Blockage of Unconfessed Sin

Wrongs against God and others that are not made right are the biggest and most threatening blockage to a pure heart. Like the tiny particles of plaque that collect in the arteries, the clog of unconfessed sin usually begins very small in the spiritual heart but grows into a major blockage. Eventually it can cut off the "blood supply" to your life, which is the flow of God's energy through His Spirit.

That's how it happened for Regina. Starting a new job, this thirty-year-old woman, whose life had been dramatically transformed by Christ only a few months earlier, had a deep desire to lead her new coworkers to Christ. But Regina also wanted desperately to succeed in her new company, where the competition for clients among the sales team was fierce.

So it didn't seem like a big deal to Regina to fudge just a bit on some numbers to make her first month's report look better. She had called on nineteen prospective new clients that month, but twenty-five looked more impressive. Besides, she would make it up the next month as she got a feel for the territory. In the meantime, Regina was developing a relationship with some of her coworkers in hopes of sharing her testimony with them when the opportunity arose.

Regina was chagrined to learn that the rest of the sales team was logging thirty to forty calls a month—at least that's what their reports showed. She reasoned that it was okay to pad her numbers until she got up to speed. After all, she had other contacts on file; she just hadn't called on them yet—and she would soon. But the dishonesty began to gnaw at her conscience. So she poured in the hours to make more calls, which gave her an excuse not to have lunch with the people in her office. She didn't feel right about sharing her newfound faith with them until she got her reports balanced out.

But with the door to her heart left ajar, Regina found it easier to make other compromises: padding her expense account, fudging on other report numbers, shading the truth with her clients to get the sale. After only a few months, not only was she avoiding her coworkers, she was skipping church and not returning phone calls and e-mails from friends in the singles group. Her small compromise had multiplied to many compromises. Regina's joy in Christ and glowing testimony had been crowded out by the accumulating blockage of sin in her heart.

God could not have made it any easier for us to remove this paralyzing blockage. The Bible says, "If we confess our sins, He is faithful and righteous to forgive us our sins and to cleanse us from all unrighteousness" (1 John 1:9). Confessing sin means to say the same thing about it that God does. We may start out by rationalizing, "It's not so bad"; but God says, "It's wrong; it's sin." We say, "Everybody else is doing it"; but God says, "It's wrong; it's sin." We say, "It will all balance out in the end"; but God says, "It's wrong; it's sin." Only when we say what God says—"It's wrong; it's sin"—can He say, "Exactly right. You're forgiven, the blockage is removed, and your heart is pure again."

Regina finally got to that point. She not only confessed to God, but she confessed to her boss what she had done and asked her forgiveness. Instead, Regina was fired. But she kept in contact with one girl in her office during the next few months as she looked for a new job. When the time seemed right, Regina told Terri what had happened. Terri asked, "Why did you apologize? It cost you your job." It was the open door Regina had been praying for. She was able to share her testimony with Terri, who is now attending the church singles group with Regina.

## The Blockage of Unresolved Anger

Emma hates her sister. When their sick mother, who had lived with Emma for several months, went to live with Trudy in another state, Trudy convinced their mom to change her last will and testament without Emma's knowledge. Trudy lied to their mom about Emma and pressured the change, which left everything of value in their mom's estate to Trudy.

When their mother died and Emma, who had become a Christian a few years earlier, discovered what had happened, she was blind with rage. Emma not only lost her part of the inheritance, but the will also designated Trudy as the recipient of their mother's personal effects and sentimental heirlooms. Emma did everything she could to unravel the web of deceit her sister had spun against her, but to no avail. Her challenge to the will's validity was denied. Her last words to Trudy after the funeral were, "I will hate you forever. I will never speak to you again. And I will do everything in my power to ruin what you have plotted so maliciously to steal from me."

There are two Greek words in the Bible for "anger." One brings to mind a flame burning a small clump of dry straw. It flares up then fades. The other word describes sustained anger, as if the person continually adds more straw to keep the blaze alive. This is brooding anger, anger you refuse to release, anger that seeks revenge. Jesus says that this kind of anger is the equivalent of murder (see Matthew 5:21–22). Anger clogs the heart of love, forgiveness, and compassion, essential components of Christ's character in us.

It took a while, but Emma's friends at church finally talked her into dealing with her anger in a healthy way instead of pouring on the fuel. Her relationship with Trudy may never be as healthy as it once was, but Emma did write a letter of apology for her venomous threats. She's hoping Trudy will someday write back.

## The Blockage of Uncontrolled Addictions

Life is often difficult and painful because we are imperfect people who live in a world of imperfect people. We sometimes get cheated, betrayed, slighted, or attacked—and it hurts. When we experience physical pain, we seek medicines from the doctor that will cure the ailment and end the pain. But when we are hurt emotionally and spiritually, we usually end up medicating ourselves in ways that temporarily numb the pain but rarely cure the malady. These self-administered "drugs" often become addictions that block the flow of God's life to our hearts.

Self-medicating can take many different forms, but the goal of all of them is to mask the pain with momentary relief or pleasure. So we go for anything that makes us feel good for a time. These "drugs" can range from actual drugs—tobacco, alcohol, marijuana, cocaine, painkillers, sleeping pills—to more socially acceptable substances like caffeine, food in general, and more harmful foods in particular. Sometimes the medication is sex when a woman seeks an illicit physical or emotional connection to soothe the pain in a troubled marriage. There are also the emotional and spiritual drugs of pop psychology, cults, psychics, and unscriptural religious experiences. As with any drug, repeated use leads to addiction; we can't function without that substance or experience.

The apostle Peter wrote, "So be content with who you are, and don't put on airs. God's strong hand is on you; he'll promote you at the right time. Live carefree before God; he is most careful with you" (1 Peter 5:7 MSG). Picture anxiety as being pulled in different directions at the same time. That sounds like real life, doesn't it? But instead of handling anxiety with self-prescribed cures that will accumulate in a blockage in the heart (both spiritually *and* physically in some cases), God invites you to give your anxiety to Him and let Him deal with it. Why? Because He cares for you and wants to save you from the additional pain your cares and supposed cures will cause you.

Giving our cares to God is not incompatible with talking to a professional counselor about these difficulties. When it comes to dealing with addictive behavior, it is healthy to have some knowledgeable, compassionate people on your team.

## The Blockage of Neglect and Indifference Toward God

Indifference toward God is Deedee's problem. She has prioritized the urgent above the most important in her life. Trying to keep up with her demanding job and a new boyfriend, she has pushed God to the margins of her life. As a result, she has drifted far from His voice of direction for her life.

Neglect and indifference toward God clog the spiritual heart. Indifference is a slow-moving process, so subtle it may not be noticed until the heart is cold toward God. You become lax at prayer, Bible study, church attendance, and fellowship with supportive Christian friends. At first, there may be a pang of guilt. Denial eases the guilt, and the heart hardens just a bit. This is followed by apathy. You just don't care about spiritual things anymore. Church is boring, and the Bible no longer makes any sense because the blockage of indifference robs your heart of understanding.

Paul wrote, "[Christ] was supreme in the beginning and—leading the resurrection parade—he is supreme in the end. From beginning to end he's there, towering far above everything, everyone" (Colossians 1:18 MSG). The antidote to the blockage of spiritual indifference is to consciously and purposefully give Christ first place in every area of your life.

## The Blockage of Idolatry

Idolatry is a major obstruction to spiritual vitality. Idolatry simply means you're serving the wrong god. How do you know if you are following the wrong god? Ask yourself two key questions.

*What do I fear above all else?* There may be an idol attached to your fears. For example, it's natural to fear the loss of a loved one, such as a husband or a child. But an unnatural fear in this area may signal that you are placing that loved one above God. And anything that can be placed in a casket should not be the object of our worship.

*What do I think about most when I don't have to think about anything else?* When the children are in bed, the dishes are done, the cat is put out, the house is quiet, and you are alone with your thoughts, what fills your mind? Do you rush to the television? A steamy romance novel? A computer game or chat room? Be careful: an idol may be tucked in there somewhere, especially if those thoughts are an obsession you can't shake!

Paul wrote in 2 Corinthians 3:18, "We all, with unveiled face, beholding as in a mirror the glory of the Lord, are being transformed into the same image from glory to glory, just as from the Lord, the Spirit." Galatians 5 describes the image into which a Christian woman is being transformed if her spiritual heart is free of idolatry: "love, joy, peace, patience, kindness, goodness, faithfulness, gentleness, self-control" (vv. 22–23). As you focus on filling your heart with the characteristics of Christ, the blockages in your heart will be dissolved.

Beginning your relationship of faith in God launches a process we call spiritual growth. Just as everything about you is coded in a tiny strand of your DNA, so your complete maturity in Christ is in your "spiritual DNA." You just need to grow into what God has already created you to be as you develop your relationship with Him. Blockages in the spiritual heart need to be removed because they impede your growth and transformation.

But as we continue to look at Christ, His nature and character are like a laser that penetrates the heart and melts the blockages. The more we focus on Jesus and His glory, the greater is the flow of spiritual transformation and power in our lives, allowing us to become like Him!

We have talked about the unique beauty of your heart and the enemies that threaten to rob you of this beauty. In part 3, we want to provide you with positive strategies for keeping your heart strong so you can be a blessing to God, to your family and friends, and to the world God has called you to serve. Drs. Duncan and Leachman begin by teaching you about the proper fuels you need for a healthy physical heart.

# Keys to Total Heart Health

## Chapter 12: Unblocking the Flow to Your Spiritual Heart

- Blockages in the spiritual heart are serious because they can shut down the flow of spiritual energy and passion for the Lord.

- Spiritual heart blockages form when the spiritual heart is blocked with foreign matter that compromises its purity, just as when the physical heart is clogged with plaque.

- *Unconfessed Sin.* Wrongs against God and others that are not made right are the most threatening blockages to a pure heart. Only when we say what God says—"It's wrong; it's sin"—and ask Him to remove our sins can the blockages be removed.

- *Unresolved Anger.* Unresolved anger blocks love, forgiveness, and compassion, essential components of Christ's character in us. We are purified of anger as we forgive others.

- *Uncontrolled Addictions.* Instead of handling our anxieties with self-prescribed cures that themselves become heart blockages, God invites us to give them to Him and let Him deal with them.

- *Neglect and Indifference Toward God.* The antidote for neglecting God is to consciously and purposefully give Christ first place in every area of your life.

- *Idolatry.* To purify yourself from idolatry, fill your heart with the characteristics of Christ.

# Part Three

The Ongoing Health
of a Woman's Heart

# 13
# Energy from the Proper Fuels

How to get more bounce in your step
with less jiggle everywhere else.

**Dr. Michael Duncan and Dr. Richard Leachman**

Energy balance is vital for a healthy physical heart. As mentioned earlier, your "energy in"—the daily calories you take in through food—should be about the same as your "energy out"—the calories you expend in daily activity. When the balance between the two is roughly even, your weight stays about the same. More energy in than energy out, and you gain weight—and run the risk of the attendant health problems. More energy out than energy in, and you lose weight. Energy balance is one of the foundations of Total Heart Health.

In this chapter and the next, we will talk about the energy-in side of the equation: a healthy diet. In order to encourage physical heart health, you need to pay attention to the kind of fuel you put into your body. In chapter 16, we will explore the energy-out side: exercise. Our recommendations on both sides will help you achieve the energy balance you desire to reach your physical health goals.

## Fuel for Your Body

You may look at your dinner plate and see a succulent grilled pork medallion, a mound of rice pilaf, a stalk of steamed broccoli, and a wedge of baked apple sprinkled with cinnamon. But what you're really looking at are the different metabolic fuels your body will use to keep you alive and functioning for the next several hours. Enjoying a delicious meal, especially in a setting of conversation with other people around a table, is one of life's more pleasant experiences. But long after the dishes are stashed in the dishwasher and your guests have gone home, your gastrointestinal system will be breaking down and sorting through that meal in search of the energy your heart must deliver to every cell in your body to keep you alive and well.

The key to the fuels you put into your body is getting the quality and quantity you need for optimum health. Too much of the wrong kinds of food—and sometimes even too much of the right kinds—and your body suffers. You won't feel as well as you could, you may not like how you look, and you run the risk of serious, life-shortening disease.

When we talk about fuels, we're talking about the three basic metabolic fuels contained in the wide variety of things we eat. Everything you eat gets broken down into three nutritional elements: fats, carbohydrates, and proteins. In a nutshell, the magnificent digestive system God created in you transforms these three fuels into the energy you need.

Since calorie count is integral to energy balance, it is important to note the number of calories in each of the three metabolic fuels. Each gram of carbohydrates contains four calories. Protein also contains about four calories per gram. Fat, however, is more energy-dense, containing nine calories per gram. This makes fat a very efficient metabolic fuel; you can go a long way on a small amount. Unfortunately for most of us, fat is *too* efficient. We usually take in more dietary fat than we burn, which means the excess goes to storage—body fat.

| Carbohydrates | 1 gram = 4 calories |
| --- | --- |
| Protein | 1 gram = 4 calories |
| Fat | 1 gram = 9 calories |

Alcohol is another energy-dense, calorie-rich food substance that weight-loss candidates sometimes overlook. Every gram of alcohol contains about seven calories. So even a glass of wine with dinner or the occasional bottle of beer piles additional calories onto the foods we eat. Furthermore, since alcohol is frequently an appetite stimulant, you may end up eating more food when alcohol is consumed with the meal. And, of course, for those people who drink more, caloric input increases proportionately.

# Facts About Fats

The fat in the food we eat is made up of chains of molecules called fatty acids. There are four major types of fatty acids, but they are not all created equal when it comes to a healthy diet. It is important to know the differences between them and how these differences can affect your energy balance. We often differentiate between the fatty acids by calling them "bad" fat—which includes saturated fatty acids and trans fatty acids—and "good" fat—which includes monounsaturated fatty acids and polyunsaturated fatty acids.

## "Bad" Fat

Saturated fatty acids are found primarily in animal fats, which is why we urge moderation—but not total abstinence—when it comes to eating red meat and dairy products such as whole milk, ice cream, butter, and cheese. Other sources of saturated fat are tropical oils such as palm oil, coconut oil, and cocoa butter.

Saturated fatty acids are a significant threat to Total Heart Health. A little bit goes a long way, and a lot can do serious damage. Saturated fat increases blood cholesterol and triglycerides, the two major fats circulating in the blood. The American Heart Association recommends that fewer than 7 percent of your total daily calories come from saturated fat.

Fish, chicken, olive oil, and canola oil are low in saturated fats, and you can chalk up zero saturated fat for nonfat dairy products, fruits, vegetables, beans, bread, and rice. The difference can be rather profound in a daily diet. Notice the comparisons of saturated-fat content below:

| | |
|---|---|
| 3.5 ounces of hamburger | 8 grams |
| 3 ounces of baked salmon | 1 gram |
| | |
| 1 tablespoon of butter | 12 grams |
| 1 tablespoon of canola oil | 1 gram |
| | |
| 1 cup of whole milk | 5 grams |
| 1 cup of nonfat milk | 0 grams |

| 3.5 ounces of fried chicken | 5 grams |
| 3.5 ounces of skinless baked chicken | 2 grams |
| | |
| 1 small slice of cheesecake | 9 grams |
| 1 large peach | 0 grams |

Trans fatty acids are the real black sheep of the dietary fat family. They are artificial fatty acids, made by hydrogenating or partially hydrogenating polyunsaturated fatty acids. You will find trans fat in processed and packaged foods requiring fat because it is more stable than polyunsaturated fat, meaning these foods don't spoil as quickly. If a packaged product contains hydrogenated or partially hydrogenated vegetable oil, then it contains trans fat. "Hydrogenated" or "partially hydrogenated" and "trans fat" mean the same thing.

Trans fatty acids seem to be a staple in junk food: packaged cookies, cakes, doughnuts, crackers, pastries, microwave popcorn, white bread, margarine, and deep-fried foods. For example, one doughnut has 3.2 grams of trans fatty acids, and a large order of fries has 6.8 grams. Foods with zero trans fat include unprocessed vegetables, fruits, grains, nuts, vegetable oils, legumes, and soy milk.

There are a lot of tempting, tasty comfort foods on the trans fat list. But beware: trans fatty acids can be trouble. There are some major adverse health problems associated with trans fatty acids. The net negative effect of trans fat on your system is about double that of saturated fat. For example, they hit you with a one-two punch in the cholesterol department. Trans fatty acids have been found to increase bad cholesterol (LDL) and decrease good cholesterol (HDL).

The preservative value of trans fat is overshadowed by its punishing effect on the heart. According to the *New England Journal of Medicine*, if you replace just 2 percent of your energy intake from trans fatty acids with monounsaturated or polyunsaturated fatty acids, you decrease the risk of coronary heart disease by a whopping 53 percent.[1]

## "Good" Fat

Monounsaturated fatty acids are one of two "good" fats. Most of the monounsaturated fatty acids are found in plants. Some prime sources are olive oil, canola oil, safflower oil, and avocados. Whenever you can replace saturated fat with monounsaturated fat, you lower your bad cholesterol without lowering your good cholesterol.

Another good fat, polyunsaturated fatty acids, are found in plant products such as sunflower oil, corn oil, flaxseed oil, pumpkin oil, walnut oil, and soybean oil and in cold-water fish such as Chinook salmon, albacore tuna, anchovy, herring, mackerel, and Pacific halibut. Polyunsaturated fatty acids are essential to ongoing good health. Since the body does not manufacture them, we must include in our diet foods that have them.

Omega-6 and omega-3 are polyunsaturated fatty acids with great benefits to heart health. Omega-6 is found in animal meat, milk, eggs, vegetable oils, seeds, and nuts. Most of us do pretty well getting omega-6 because its sources are common menu items in most homes. Omega-3 is found in leafy green vegetables, flax, flaxseed oil, canola oil, walnuts, Brazil nuts, fish, and fish oil.

Medical research is discovering some wonderful heart benefits from omega-3, and eating fish significantly factors into the results. One study tracked eighty-five thousand women over a sixteen-year period. Those who ate fish at least once a week experienced a 30 percent lower risk of heart disease. And women who ate fish at least five times a week lowered their risk by 45 percent.[2]

A study of twenty-two thousand men over a seventeen-year span revealed similar results. Men with the highest level of omega-3 in their blood were 80 percent less likely to experience sudden death.[3] In an Italian study of eleven thousand male heart-attack survivors, those assigned to take fish oil supplements daily were 53 percent less likely to die suddenly than those assigned to take a placebo.[4] And omega-3 works just as well for women.

So when it comes to dietary fat for you and your family, don't overlook the polyunsaturated varieties, especially omega-3. Plan cold-water fish into your weekly menu. The payoff will be a decreased risk of sudden cardiac death, arrhythmia, elevated blood triglyceride levels, and blood clots.

## Total Heart Health Recommendation for Fats

When it comes to fat, our recommendations for Total Heart Health will be fairly obvious to most people, but here they are:

*Decrease saturated fat.* We're not suggesting that you completely give up steaks and other red meats. But instead of ordering a Texas-sized Porterhouse when you go out, select a six-ounce cut of lean beef or fish instead. If you treat yourself to a burger, get one with a single patty instead of two or three. When buying ground beef at the market, select packages with a lower fat content. Also, cut back on dairy products or go with low-fat or nonfat varieties.

*Greatly decrease trans fat.* Ideally, we would be better off to eliminate consumption of trans fat. But it would be difficult for most of us, because trans fat is in so many of the packaged food products we buy at the market. Careful monitoring is the key. It won't kill you to have an occasional Oreo or two, but if you can't stop with one or two, don't bring them into the house. The same goes for other packaged baked goods. Also, cut way back on fried foods. For example, grill or broil your chicken and fish instead of frying it in a skillet or deep-frying it. Relegate French fries to a rare treat in your diet instead of a weekly staple.

*Replace saturated fat and trans fat with monounsaturated and polyunsaturated fat.* Instead of using spreads like butter or margarine, try dipping your bread in olive oil and herbs like we do in Italian restaurants. Include vegetable oils, nuts, flaxseed, and flaxseed oil in your diet. And most important of all, eat fish, such as cold-water salmon (not farm-raised) and water-packed albacore tuna (not oil-packed). You may even consider fish oil supplements to maximize the benefits of omega-3.

## Clues About Carbs

Another major metabolic fuel is carbohydrates. Starches are the major carbohydrates in most diets: bread, beans, rice, pasta, potatoes, corn, and so on. Carbohydrates are essentially sugars. There are three basic types of carbohydrates in a normal diet: starches, which are the major type; sucrose, which is table sugar; and lactose, which is the main sugar found in milk products. During the digestive process, starch, sucrose, and lactose are broken down into the elemental sugar molecules of fructose, glucose, and galactose, which are absorbed into the bloodstream and burned as energy.

Glucose is vitally important to all metabolism. It is the universal fuel for all human cells. Your muscles need glucose for physical activity, which is why athletes need high levels of carbohydrates in their training diet. The brain and red blood cells rely heavily on glucose as a primary fuel source. The brain can at times operate on other types of fuels, but your red blood cells are 100 percent dependent on glucose for their function.

Carbohydrates are generally grouped under two headings—simple and complex.

## Simple Carbohydrates

Simple carbohydrates can be easily broken down and absorbed in the intestinal tract to provide energy in a hurry. You want simple carbs when your blood sugar is plummeting and you need a quick energy boost. Examples of simple carbs are fruit juices, soft drinks, and refined foods such as white bread, white rice (especially the instant variety), potatoes, and certain types of crackers and cereals.

Simple carbs deliver needed calories quickly, but they provide little else in the way of nutrients the body needs. That's why the calories from simple carbs are often referred to as "empty calories." And that's why you are more likely to be hungry sooner after eating simple carbs than after eating complex carbs.

We use sweeteners of various types to make food taste better, and most of these sweeteners are simple carbohydrates—sugars. There are two kinds of sweeteners: nutritive and non-nutritive. Nutritive means it has caloric value and little else—empty calories. Some examples are table sugar, honey, fructose, and brown sugar—which is nothing more than table sugar flavored with molasses. Non-nutritive sweeteners are most commonly found in those little pink, blue, and yellow packets many people use at mealtimes in place of sugar. These powdery sugar substitutes, which are up to seven hundred times sweeter than table sugar, are made from amino acids, aspartic acids, and phenylalanine. Non-nutritive sweeteners are an acceptable option for adding a sweet taste without adding calories. But stay informed about the possible disadvantages of non-nutritive sweeteners.

## Complex Carbohydrates

We also need complex carbohydrates, which provide calories while also supplying nutritional elements such as vitamins, minerals, fat, fiber, protein, phytochemicals, and antioxidants. Complex carbs are found in foods such as whole-grain breads, oatmeal, peas, lentils, beans, whole fruits (instead of juices), and brown rice (instead of white rice). Complex carbs take longer to process in the digestive system, but they provide more of the nutrients we need and help forestall feelings of hunger.

Any glucose in your system you don't use up in activity and exercise is stored in limited amounts in the liver and muscle in a complex called glycogen. Once those storage facilities are full, additional glucose is packaged into fat particles and transported to adipose tissue in the body for storage. So the key is to limit carbohydrate intake so that only a minimal amount is stored as fat.

## Total Heart Health Recommendations for Carbohydrates

Our Total Heart Health recommendations will again seem rather obvious once this basic information is understood.

*Decrease intake of simple carbohydrates.* Cut back on table sugar and honey on cereal, in coffee and tea, and in other uses. Non-nutritive sweeteners are an alternative to consider, but ask your doctor first about the potential negative effects in the sweeteners you use. If you're a meat-and-potatoes kind of person, reduce your portions of potatoes and/or substitute other vegetables. And draw a decisive line in the sand when it comes to sweets like cookies, cakes, and sugary soft drinks, rationing out to yourself only a modest amount.

*Increase intake of complex carbohydrates.* Eat plenty of fresh vegetables and fruits. When you eat breads and cereals, make sure they are the whole-grain variety. And include adequate amounts of fiber, healthy fats, and protein in your daily diet.

# Points About Protein

Protein is the third major metabolic fuel. Unlike fat and the glucose from carbohydrates, your body cannot store amino acids. So you need amino acids and protein in your diet every day. A healthy diet requires about one gram of protein per kilogram (2.2 pounds) of body weight—and we're talking about your ideal weight according to the body mass index. Women generally require about fifty grams of protein per day, while men require about sixty-five grams. Most of us equate protein with meat. But there are other very good sources of protein you can work into your diet that won't elevate your saturated fat intake as meat does. Here are several examples, compared to the protein in meat:

| | | |
|---|---|---|
| Meat, poultry, fish | 4 ounces cooked (90 grams) | 28 grams protein |
| Milk or yogurt | 1 cup | 8 grams protein |
| Egg | 1 medium | 7 grams protein |
| Cheese | 2 slices (60 grams) | 14 grams protein |
| Legumes | 1 cup | 7 grams protein |
| Peanut butter | 2 tablespoons | 14 grams protein |

There is a definite weight-control benefit to increased protein in the diet. The stomach empties slower with protein due to the prolonged digestion process. As a result, nutrient absorption is slowed and you will feel full longer, meaning you may not be as tempted to snack between meals. But remember: if you rely heavily on red meat for your protein needs, you will be loading up on saturated fat, which negates the weight-loss benefit.

When it comes to sources of dietary protein, there are two types: *complete* protein and *incomplete* protein.

## Complete Protein

Foods with complete protein contain all the essential amino acids, and foods with incomplete protein lack some essential amino acids. Generally speaking, animal protein is complete protein, so a reasonable amount of meat and eggs in your diet is okay. A lot of people equate protein with red meat, which is loaded with saturated fat and cholesterol. But there are other sources of protein. Fish is an excellent source of protein as well as omega-3 fatty acid, so you are doing your body a lot of good when you eat fish.

## Incomplete Protein

Plant protein tends to be incomplete protein because most foods from plants are missing some essential amino acids. Sources of plant protein include whole grains, nuts, beans, and other legumes. Soy has been a hot diet topic in the last few years because it is the only plant that is a complete protein. In addition to all the amino acids, soy offers a number of health benefits. Fortified soy products are an excellent source of vitamins $B_{12}$ and D, and soy may lower bad cholesterol. Soy may also reduce the risk of cancer and osteoporosis and the symptoms of menopause in some women. But there may be some adverse neurological effects of soy, so we recommend using soy products in moderation.

## Total Heart Health Recommendations for Protein

Our Total Heart Health recommendations for protein intake include the following:

*Increase plant sources of protein.* Take advantage of protein sources such as beans, nuts, and whole grains.

*Eat more fish.* Fish, especially the cold-water variety, is doubly beneficial. It is an excellent source of protein, and it supplies valuable omega-3 fatty acids.

*Moderate the intake of beef and dairy products.* Smaller portions of lean beef are better for most people than giving up meat altogether. And when you include dairy products, go for low-fat or nonfat varieties.

*Avoid high-protein diets.* In chapter 18, we will discuss many of the diet fads on the scene today and highlight their strengths and weaknesses. But the bottom line for most of them, including high protein, is that a balanced approach to nutrition is better.

In the next chapter, we will continue this discussion of dietary fuels by exploring items such as cholesterol, fiber, vitamins, and minerals.

# Keys to Total Heart Health

## Chapter 13: Energy from the Proper Fuels

- Fuels for your body are fats, carbohydrates, and proteins, which your digestive system, created magnificently by God, processes into energy.

- "Bad" fat is made up of saturated and trans fatty acids. Saturated fats are found in animal fats. Trans fatty acids are found in processed and packaged foods requiring fat.

- Monounsaturated and polyunsaturated fatty acids are "good" fats. Most monounsaturated fatty acids are found in plants. Polyunsaturated fatty acids are in plant products and in cold-water fish.

- We recommend you decrease saturated fat, greatly decrease trans fat, and replace saturated and trans fat with monounsaturated and polyunsaturated fat.

- Carbs are grouped as simple and complex. Simple carbs deliver needed calories quickly but provide little nutrition. Complex carbs provide calories and supply vitamins, minerals, fat, fiber, protein, phytochemicals, and antioxidants.

- We recommend you decrease your intake of simple carbohydrates and increase your intake of complex carbohydrates.

- Proteins are classified as complete and incomplete. Complete protein foods—like meat and eggs—have all essential amino acids. Incomplete protein foods—like plant foods—lack some of the essential amino acids.

- We recommend you increase plant sources of protein, eat more fish, moderate the intake of beef and dairy products, and avoid high-protein diets.

## 1 4
# Adding Fire to Dietary Fuels

Cholesterol, fiber, vitamins, minerals—
and what they mean in your daily diet.
**Dr. Michael Duncan and Dr. Richard Leachman**

Fats, proteins, and carbohydrates are the major components of the metabolic fuels you need for daily energy. But there are a lot of other dietary health terms floating around that you may be wondering about. Let's talk about several of them and learn how they can help or hinder heart health.

## Cholesterol and Triglycerides: Traveling Companions

Cholesterol and triglycerides are the two major fats circulating in the bloodstream. Cholesterol is not strictly a nutritional issue, but it is an important health issue that is often talked about with fat, so let's look at it more closely.

### Cholesterol

Cholesterol is a fat, and most of the cholesterol in your body is manufactured by your liver. The cholesterol in the food you eat does not necessarily translate one-to-one to the amount of cholesterol circulating in your bloodstream. But you do want to monitor your cholesterol intake and do what you can to keep your blood cholesterol within healthy limits.

We have already learned about the two types of cholesterol. LDL is "bad" cholesterol, and HDL is "good" cholesterol. Few people can remember which is which, so you might think of them by their first letters: LDL can make your life *lousy*, and HDL can make your life *happy*. LDL in the bloodstream accumulates on the walls of the arteries as plaque, which can, over time, result in blood clots, blockage in the arteries, and possibly a heart attack. HDL in the bloodstream actually carries away some of the LDL particles and has been known to cause a reduction in plaque buildup or atherosclerosis.

So HDL and LDL are kind of like the cops and robbers of the circulatory system. When LDL is rampant, you've got big trouble brewing. As we learned when talking about fats, trans fatty acids in your diet can induce a cholesterol "crime spree" in your bloodstream, increasing LDL while decreasing HDL. But when HDL is on the job in force, it can greatly reduce cholesterol "crime" in your arteries. So it is important to do whatever you can to decrease LDL while increasing HDL.

It is now recommended that your total cholesterol be no greater than 200 mg/dl. As for LDL, if you have fewer than two risk factors (diabetes, smoking, hypertension, family history, low HDL), your bad cholesterol should be no higher than 160 mg/dl. If you have two or more risk factors, your LDL should be no greater than 130 mg/dl. And if you have been diagnosed with coronary artery disease, your LDL should be kept at 70 or less.

As for HDL, we mentioned earlier that women tend to have higher levels of HDL than men do. So an HDL value of 45 mg/dl or higher is normal for women, while 35 mg/dl is the normal range for men.

There are two known ways to beef up the "police force" of HDL in your bloodstream. The first is regular exercise. The second, which is still under some debate, is alcohol. Some doctors and nutritionists today recommend one to two drinks three to five days per week. Consult your doctor or nutritionist for the latest data on this topic as well as for treatment options.

## Triglycerides

Triglyceride is the other major fat in your bloodstream. Elevated triglyceride levels can contribute to development of coronary artery disease, but high levels are a less potent predictor of CAD than cholesterol. Persons with excessively high triglyceride levels are at risk to develop pancreatitis—severe inflammation of the pancreas.

Elevated triglycerides have also been associated with the metabolic syndrome, which is comprised of a group of metabolic risks found in an individual. A person with metabolic syndrome characteristically suffers from all of the following: central obesity, or excessive fat tissue around the midsection; high triglycerides and low HDL, contributing to plaque buildup in the arteries; insulin resistance or glucose intolerance; diabetes; and elevated blood pressure. This syndrome predisposes the patient to cardiovascular disease.

Elevated triglycerides are dramatically corrected by reducing the intake of carbohydrates and sugars. While there are certain genetic aberrations that can lead to elevated triglycerides, the overwhelming majority of these patients are obese and/or suffer from diabetes. Once again, poor diet and eating habits are at the root of the problem, and changing those habits and embracing a Total Heart Health lifestyle can help reverse them.

## Dietary Fiber: Making the Most of Your Meals

Dietary fiber is a plant substance that is virtually indigestible. In other words, the fiber you get in the foods you eat travels entirely through your intestinal tract without being absorbed into the system as fats, carbohydrates, and proteins are. Most fiber is a complex carbohydrate that the body cannot break down.

There are two classifications of fiber: soluble and insoluble. Both are necessary to digestion and health.

### Soluble Fiber

Soluble fiber is found in foods that contain ingredients like oat bran, pectin, psyllium, legumes, guar gum, mucilages, and citrucell. If the last two words look familiar, it's probably because you have seen fiber supplements in the drug aisle of your supermarket with similar brand names: Metamucil and Citrucel. In a normal diet, you gain the benefits of soluble fiber from such foods as oatmeal, barley, beans, lentils, apples, pears, bananas, citrus fruits, and Brussels sprouts.

The soluble fiber in your food forms a gel in the stomach and small intestine as digestion begins. This gel expands in the stomach and slows emptying, allowing you to feel full longer, which may help you cut down on between-meal snacks. The gel continues to move slowly through the small intestine, allowing for slower absorption of nutrients and bile salts from your food. And since digestion is moving in slow motion, carbs are not as rapidly broken down and absorbed, which keeps your glycemic index in a healthier range.

As the mass moves through the large intestine or colon, it undergoes further fermentation by bacteria, which extracts elements useful to the body's immune system and for fighting cancer, particularly in the colon.

## Insoluble Fiber

Insoluble fiber is found in foods containing wheat bran, sterculia, mignin, and methyl cellulose. You get your insoluble fiber from eating whole-wheat products: wheat, oat, and corn bran; flaxseed; vegetables such as green beans and cauliflower, and the skins of fruit and root vegetables such as potatoes.

The effect of insoluble fiber is focused less on the stomach and small intestine and more on the colon in the digestive process. It helps slow transit time and increases water absorption in the stool. Insoluble fiber also performs what some have called a mop-and-sponge effect by cleaning up potential toxins left over in the intestinal tract.

Fiber is thought to protect against colon cancer, and it is useful in treating constipation, diverticular disease, irritable bowel syndrome, and hemorrhoids. We recommend twenty to thirty grams of dietary fiber per day. The average American diet contains only about fifteen grams, so most of us fall short. The best way to remedy this shortfall is to add more fruits, vegetables, and whole-grain products to your daily menu. You can up your fiber intake, for example, by eating whole-grain breads. A slice of refined-wheat bread has about one gram of fiber, but a slice of whole-grain bread has two to four grams.

Try adding fiber at breakfast. Start with a bowl of whole-grain cereal. For example, a small packet of instant oatmeal gives you about four grams of fiber. You can find other whole-grain cereals with up to ten grams per serving. And don't overlook the fiber advantage in beans—pinto beans, kidney beans, lima beans, navy beans, or black beans, which are high in dietary fiber. You may also want to take a fiber supplement to make sure you're getting enough.

# Vitamins and Minerals:
## Make Sure You're Firing on All Cylinders

Vitamins and minerals are the essential micronutrients for heart health. There are about forty of them we must purposely take in through the food we eat or through vitamin supplements, because the body cannot manufacture these elements. The four categories are water-soluble vitamins, fat-soluble vitamins, major minerals, and trace minerals.

## Water-Soluble Vitamins

Water-soluble vitamins are all the B vitamins as well as vitamin C, also known as ascorbic acid. They are listed below, along with how much of each we need daily. You need far less of the vitamins measured in micrograms (mcg) than those measured in milligrams (mg).

| B Vitamins | 100% US RDA |
|---|---|
| Thiamine (vitamin $B_1$) | 1.5 mg |
| Riboflavin (vitamin $B_2$) | 1.7 mg |
| Pyridoxine (vitamin $B_6$) | 2.0 mg |
| Niacin (vitamin $B_3$) | 20 mg |
| Folic acid (folate) | 400 mcg |
| Pantothenic acid | 10 mg |
| Cobalamine (vitamin $B_{12}$) | 6 mg |
| Biotin | 300 mcg |
| **Vitamin C** (ascorbic acid) | 60 mg |

They are called water soluble because they are found in the watery portion of food. You need thiamine, riboflavin, niacin, pantothenic acid, and biotin to free energy from your food into your bloodstream. Pyridoxine, cobalamine, and folic acid help metabolize protein and amino acids and are useful in the synthesis of collagen, which is the support structure of the body.

Vitamin C is an antioxidant that is necessary for collagen synthesis, providing skin tone. Vitamin C does not prevent the common cold, but it prevents scurvy and is thought to reduce risk of cancer of the mouth, esophagus, stomach, and breast. Good sources of vitamin C are citrus fruits, bell peppers, spinach, tomatoes, and broccoli.

Folic acid is extremely important to pregnant women, especially during the early stages of pregnancy. Folate is necessary for new cell creation, and it reduces the risk of brain and spinal defects in the developing fetus.

Natural sources include fortified grains, cereals, okra, spinach, orange and tomato juices, turnip greens, and broccoli. *Folic acid supplements, such as in multivitamins, should be taken by all women of childbearing age.* You need at least 400 micrograms per day.

Vitamin $B_{12}$ has been shown to decrease levels of homocysteine, a compound associated with heart disease. Deficiency of vitamin $B_{12}$ can lead to anemia, some neurological diseases, heart disease, and cancer. Good sources include meat, fish, poultry, fortified cereals, eggs, and soy milk.

Generally speaking, it is difficult to get too much of the water-soluble vitamins because the kidneys will flush out what you cannot use. So it's no problem if you forget and take your B and C vitamins twice in the same day. Pyridoxine is the exception and could result in nerve damage. But it is rare for someone to accidentally overdose on it.

## Fat-Soluble Vitamins

Here are the fat-soluble vitamins and their daily allowances. We recommend that most people aim for the higher range of vitamin D because many people are deficient in that vitamin. Notice that three of the four vitamins are measured in international units (IU), while vitamin K is measured in micrograms (mcg).

|  | 100% US RDA |
|---|---|
| **Vitamin D** | 400–600 IU |
| **Vitamin E** | 30 IU or 15 mg |
| **Vitamin A** | 5,000 IU or 700 mg |
| **Vitamin K** | 120 mcg men |
|  | 90 mcg women |

The fat-soluble vitamins, which come as fatty acids or oils, are absorbed into the lymphatic system, where they are stored in fat or in the liver until your body needs them. Since your body can store them up, there is potential for toxicity with overdoses of these vitamins, so you want to stay close to the recommended daily dosage.

Vitamin A is important for good vision, bone growth, and healthy skin. Sources include beef (especially liver), eggs, and cheese. Beta carotene can also be converted to vitamin A. You get beta carotene in carrots, sweet potatoes, pumpkins, squash, and turnip greens.

Vitamin D is important for calcium and phosphorus metabolism and for healthy bone structure and teeth. You can get vitamin D through salmon, eggs, and fortified foods such as milk and cereals. Vitamin D is also increased through the skin's exposure to ultraviolet-B radiation from sunlight. Adequate levels of vitamin D reduce the risk of colon cancer. Deficiency results in osteoporosis, osteomalacia, rickets, and musculoskeletal pain. The best way to ensure that you are getting at least 400 IU daily is through a vitamin D supplement.

Vitamin E is an antioxidant that may help decrease the risk of Alzheimer's disease when it is combined with vitamin C. But contrary to what some beauty products promise, vitamin E does not prevent wrinkles. Natural sources include vegetable oils, whole grains, nuts, and leafy green vegetables.

Vitamin K is essential for blood clotting. People on blood thinners need to be careful about taking a vitamin K supplement because it may interfere with the anticoagulation properties of the drug. Natural sources of vitamin K include green vegetables, cabbage, milk, and eggs.

## Major Minerals and Trace Minerals

The major minerals needed for daily health are sodium, potassium, chloride, calcium, phosphorous, magnesium, and sulfur. Sodium, potassium, and chloride are very important for maintaining proper water and electrolyte balance in your body. Calcium, phosphorus, and magnesium are vital to a healthy bone structure. And sulfur is needed to stabilize protein structure.

We have all been cautioned about the amount of dietary sodium—salt—in our diet. The average American consumes about 4,000 milligrams of salt daily. Government guidelines used to recommend up to 2,400 milligrams daily, but the recommendation has recently been dropped to 1,500. There seems to be an abundance of sodium in most of the foods we eat, so it's a good idea to look for ways to cut back on our use of salt.

Trace minerals, as you might guess from the term, are found in very small quantities in the body. Some of the more common ones are chromium, copper, fluoride, iodine, iron, manganese, selenium, and zinc. Check the label on your bottle of multivitamins for a number of others. But these minerals are absolutely essential for a variety of tasks. Iodine, for example, is used in the thyroid gland to make thyroid hormones. Iron is used to make your red blood cells. Manganese and other trace minerals are used as cofactors in enzyme reactions.

Some women are diligent about planning menus to meet the daily vitamin and mineral needs for themselves and their families. But we find that most women are just too busy to assure that they are eating a completely nutritional diet. We believe the cost-to-benefit ratio of taking daily supplements of vitamins and minerals just makes good sense. These days you can buy dietary supplements that are made specifically for women and targeted to your age group. As always, check with your doctor to make sure your selection of supplements is right for you.

## Water: How Much Is Enough?

It seems like everywhere you go you see people sipping from plastic bottles of water. From the gym to the workplace to the car to the refrigerator in the average home, water bottles abound. The brand name on the label and the style of plastic bottle people prefer are almost a fashion statement these days. Many people started buying water at the supermarket in case lots simply because "everybody else is doing it."

This is one popular trend in our culture that is very good for us. Water is an essential nutrient for optimum cell function in the body. Without sufficient quantities of water, the body suffers from dehydration. Too much water can result in a condition called water intoxication. Fortunately, the kidneys are quite efficient at regulating large variations in water consumption without allowing disease states.

As a general rule, you need one milliliter of water per day for each calorie of energy you expend. In other words, multiply your calorie-need profile by 0.001 to find your daily water need in liters. For example, if you are a moderately active woman burning 2,200 calories a day in your activity, you should be drinking about 2.2 liters of water a day (2,200 x 0.001).[1] That translates to about six twelve-ounce glasses of water. And if you are very active, such as playing sports or working out aggressively, you may want to up your intake to make sure you are properly hydrated for good heart health.

Your heart's health and your body's energy depend on the quality and quantity of fuels you take into your body. The same can be said about the health and vitality of your spiritual heart. Dr. and Mrs. Young will now help you understand how to maximize spiritual heart health through the energy provided by spiritual "fuels."

# Keys to Total Heart Health

## Chapter 14: Adding Fire to Dietary Fuels

- Cholesterol and triglycerides are the two major fats circulating in the bloodstream.

- LDL is "bad" cholesterol, and HDL is "good" cholesterol.

- There are two ways to beef up the "police force" of HDL in your bloodstream—regular exercise and alcohol. There is debate about alcohol, and you should consult your doctor or nutritionist for the latest data.

- Elevated triglyceride levels contribute to development of coronary artery disease and increase risk of pancreatitis. Elevated triglycerides are dramatically corrected by reducing intake of sugars and carbohydrates.

- Fiber is thought to protect against colon cancer and is useful in treating constipation, diverticular disease, irritable bowel syndrome, and hemorrhoids.

- We recommend twenty to thirty grams of dietary fiber per day through fruits, vegetables, and whole-grain products. Try adding fiber at breakfast.

- Water-soluble vitamins are all the B vitamins and vitamin C. They are found in the watery portion of food. Fat-soluble vitamins come as fatty acids or oils, and include vitamins D, E, A, K.

- Major minerals needed daily are sodium, potassium, chloride, calcium, phosphorous, magnesium, and sulfur. Trace minerals are found in small quantities in the body— chromium, copper, fluoride, iodine, iron, manganese, selenium, and zinc.

- Water is an essential nutrient to the body for allowing the proper environment for optimum cell function.

# 15
## Spiritual Energy
## for Every Hour of the Day

Enjoy God as you never have before,
no matter how tough your life is.

**Ed and Jo Beth Young**

Candace and Josh have been married for fifteen years, and they have three active kids, ages seven, ten, and thirteen. Candace is a stay-at-home mom while Josh puts in long hours as the breadwinner. It's a wildly busy life for this mother—daily carpool to and from school, meal preparation, seemingly endless laundry duty, and after-school homework to help with or correct. Yet Candace still finds time to serve as a volunteer in their community's senior center. She's also on the board of their neighborhood association. And she has recently started work on a master's degree.

On the surface, Candace looks like Wonder Woman, causing some of her friends to wonder if she is running on fumes physically, emotionally, and spiritually. How long can she keep up this pace? Will one more responsibility or crisis push her over the edge? To be sure, Candace's life is perpetually demanding, hectic, and stressful.

But this thirty-eight-year-old wife and mother is not only surviving; she's thriving. She has a strong, healthy heart, and she is growing stronger in every respect. Her friends count on her emotional support, and Josh acknowledges that Candace is a living example of the Proverbs 31 woman.

How can a woman like Candace thrive in a whirlwind existence when others, some with much less on their plate, seem to wither under the pressure? The answer is spiritual energy balance. Candace expends tons of physical, emotional, and spiritual energy keeping her marriage, family, and service to others

151

functioning and fruitful. If she fails to replenish her supply of "fuel," she will crash and burn. Sadly, that's what is happening to many women today who are racing to meet the demands of family, career, church, and social life. But Candace thrives because she takes in plenty of energy to fuel her busy life. That's energy balance: taking in enough energy to adequately compensate for the energy you expend.

In this chapter, Jo Beth and I want to talk about energy balance for the spiritual heart, specifically how to maintain the energy level you need to thrive spiritually. Energy in focuses on a healthy spiritual "diet." Then in chapter 17, we will coach you on how to get the spiritual "exercise" you need to achieve proper energy balance.

## Running on High Energy

Just a glimpse at the life of Jesus reveals that He expended tremendous energy day by day in His ministry of teaching and healing. For example, when Jesus was touched by the woman with the hemorrhage, He felt power leaving Him (see Mark 5:25–34). Imagine the power drained from Jesus's body every day as He ministered to the needy crowds who thronged around Him. Yes, He was God, but He was God wrapped in human flesh. He got hungry and weary just like we do. Where did He get the energy to meet the great spiritual demand on Him?

The Gospels record that Jesus prepared for His ministry with prayer, often rising long before sunrise to seek out a secluded spot to commune with His Father. We also learn that it was His custom to be in the synagogue on the Sabbath to worship and read from the Old Testament scrolls (see Luke 4:16). If Jesus needed "energy in" to nurture His spiritual heart and equip Him for the "energy out" of ministry, how much more do we?

Being a pastor, I know what it feels like to be spiritually drained. After a long Sunday of preaching and ministry, you can knock on me and hear nothing but an echo because I feel so empty. Your situation may not be quite the same, but you know what it means to sense the spiritual and emotional energy being sucked from you as the day goes by. It may be the stress of working at a job with a grouchy boss and whining coworkers. It may be a stressful home situation, conflicts in the neighborhood or at church, demanding relatives, or needy friends.

The key to energy balance for Jesus was knowing how to replenish His energy. Jesus purposely energized Himself in the Father's presence, and as He did, He was more than a match for the demands of His ministry. We want to share with you several essential principles for spiritual energy balance. It all starts with "energy in," receiving from God the fuel you need to nurture a strong spiritual heart.

## Start the Day with a Full Tank

In order to keep up her demanding pace, Candace rises at five every morning for a time of personal prayer and Bible reading. It's the only time of the day she consistently has to herself. Since she's up so early, most evenings Candace falls into bed exhausted before nine thirty. But she feels unprepared for each day unless she fuels her spiritual tank first thing. We encourage you to set aside time at the beginning of your day—even rising thirty minutes earlier if necessary—to spend with God. You will be amazed at the positive difference it will make in your daily life.

We have learned the value of starting each day with prayer. My first routine upon rising is to kneel beside the bed and pray. Often I use an acrostic to help me stay on track as I pray: the letters SELF. These four letters remind me how important it is to bring my*self* to God as the day begins. If it is difficult for you to focus your thoughts first thing in the morning, I recommend this simple outline to you. It need only take a moment or two. Here's how it works.

*S* is for *surrender*. Paul urged believers to present their bodies to God as a living and holy sacrifice (see Romans 12:1), so I offer myself to God in complete surrender at the beginning of the day. I ask for and yield to His agenda above my own. Surrender doesn't mean you become invisible. Rather, by surrendering to God you put yourself at His disposal to become His highly visible and useful instrument in the world.

*E* is for *empty*. Jesus said, "Self-sacrifice is the way, my way, to finding yourself, your true self" (Matthew 16:24 MSG). Self-sacrifice means emptying myself of anything that could interrupt the flow of God's energy into my life.

This is the time in my prayer when I confess my sin, weakness, and inadequacy and receive God's forgiveness according to 1 John 1:9.

*L* is for *lift*. Next, I spend a few moments lifting my praise and worship to God. Worship in the Bible is often associated with the physical posture of lifting up to God. The Psalms urge us to lift up our voices, our heads, our hearts, and our hands to God in worship and adoration. As you lift yourself up to God, you are in perfect position to receive the outpouring of the energy you need.

*F* is for *fill*. Ephesians 5:18 commands us, "Be filled with the Spirit." Having surrendered to God's agenda, emptied myself of every hindrance, and lifted my heart to God in worship, I ask the Holy Spirit to fill my life completely. This is what it means to tap into God's energy supply.

And notice the promising results of this infilling: "Speaking to one another in psalms and hymns and spiritual songs, singing and making melody with your heart to the Lord [instead of harping, criticizing, blaming, snipping, and gossiping]; always giving thanks for all things [instead of whining, grousing, complaining, and murmuring] in the name of our Lord Jesus Christ to God, even the Father" (vv. 19–20). Will your day be more productive and fruitful as you draw on the energy of the Spirit? Absolutely!

The Word of God is another essential element for filling your spiritual tank. You may not have time for a lengthy Bible study every morning. But at least spend a few moments in the Word, such as reading and meditating on a few verses, listening to a devotional on tape or on the radio, or memorizing or reciting Bible passages as you drive to work.

## Recognize That You Are Important to God

Jesus recognized everyone's importance. On His way to the home of a synagogue official to heal his desperately ill daughter, Jesus was touched by a woman who needed healing from a persistent hemorrhage. In that culture, women were treated as inferior, and perhaps this woman was only a lowly peasant. In contrast to the synagogue official's needs, her needs may have been judged by the throng to be unworthy of the Master's attention. Yet Jesus interrupted His journey to minister to this woman, even addressing her as "daughter" (Mark 5:34).

You may be underpaid at work, underappreciated at home, or undervalued in other circles. But take strength in the fact that you are more important to God than you can imagine. In fact, God is looking for people just like you, people who are open to His energy. Second Chronicles 16:9 says, "For the eyes of the LORD move to and fro throughout the earth that He may strongly support those whose heart is completely His."

## Be the Prayer Warrior God Made You to Be

When it comes to dealing with obstacles and stresses in your life, prayer is your God-given "weapon of mass destruction." Paul writes in Ephesians 6:12, "Our struggle is not against flesh and blood, but against the rulers, against the powers, against the world forces of this darkness, against the spiritual forces of wickedness in the heavenly places." Prayer is how you get through the skirmishes, conflicts, and battles of daily life. John Piper writes, "Until we know that life is war, we won't know what prayer is for."[1] When you pray, you bring God's power to bear on the spiritual forces set against you and against God's purposes in your life.

Sometimes we try to fight the battle with the wrong weapons. We assume we can change things by human tactics, ranging from a sharp corrective word to a violent physical outburst. Trying to win spiritual battles through human means doesn't work. Spiritual conflicts are fought in the spiritual realm, and it takes energized prayer to wage such a battle.

The honest truth is, women are flat-out better pray-ers than men. Some of the most powerful praying people of history have been women. Evelyn Christenson, author of the best-selling *What Happens When Women Pray*, says her mother was "the greatest pray-er I have ever known."[2] Church growth expert C. Peter Wagner says that some 80 percent of people identifying themselves as disciplined, consistent pray-ers are women.[3] This reality is corroborated by secular studies, such as one conducted by Anne McCaffrey of the Harvard Medical School, who found that "women pray more than men."[4] While God is just as tuned in to a man's prayers as to a woman's, women seem to possess greater sensitivity to the importance of prayer.

You need to take seriously your role as a pray-er. Throughout the day, be in constant prayer for your husband, your children, your boss, your coworkers, your friends, and even your opponents. Approach every opportunity, conversation, and conflict with prayer. Pray as you drive, cook, clean, work, and bathe the children. Spend several moments each day bowed in focused prayer, then sustain that conversation with God even through the busiest moments with quick sentence prayers while you're on the go. Consider implementing different types of fasting; prayer and fasting are a biblical pattern. When you pray, you are a conduit for God's energy to meet the needs around you.

## Offer Even Your Mundane Tasks as Service to God

When Candace surveys her week, she discovers that little she does could be considered glamorous or exciting. It's mostly housework, childcare, and school-work. And apart from church on Sunday, daily quiet time, and weekly women's Bible study, nothing else she does seems very "spiritual."

Candace doesn't consider herself a candidate to succeed Mother Teresa, Margaret Thatcher, or Condoleezza Rice. She'll make no speeches at the United Nations or solve the Middle East crisis. But Candace reminds herself continually to view all of her tasks as opportunities to serve God. One of her favorite memory verses is 1 Corinthians 10:31: "Do everything . . . heartily and freely to God's glory" (MSG). She finds that when she devotes her efforts to God as an act of worship, the energy she needs from Him to follow through with the task is always there.

Do the mundane duties of your day drain you instead of energize you? Maybe you need to change your primary motivation. Sure, the laundry still needs to get folded and the litter box must be cleaned out. But what if you dedicated these tasks to the glory of God and did them to please Him? It will make a tremendous difference in both your motivation and your energy level!

So whatever you must do—file papers, hammer out reports on the computer keyboard, wash dishes, change diapers, argue a case in court—do it for Him. You will experience the satisfaction of knowing your effort is bringing glory to God.

## Use Your Spiritual Energy for Earthly Good

Pursuing God's energy doesn't mean you must be a recluse. Strike a balance between your times of quiet solitude and busy service to others, between activities of private inspiration and social engagement. Some Christians become so heavenly minded they are of little earthly good. Rather than walking in a spiritually energized relationship with God and the people around them, they retreat into a kind of Christian mysticism. "Worldly" responsibilities such as caring for family and earning a living are viewed as bothersome interruptions to such "heavenly" pursuits as Bible conferences, church meetings, and personal studies.

Yes, you need to spend time nurturing your body, soul, and spirit. But if you use "spirituality" as an excuse to marginalize or ignore others, you are misusing the energy God has placed at your disposal. God doesn't fill you with His Spirit just so you can be spiritually fat and happy; He pours His energy into you to empower you for service to others. Move toward a good balance between personal nurturing and ministering to the needs of others.

## Your Life Is Worth Duplicating

One of the finest tributes to Christian women in the Bible is given by Paul in a letter to his spiritual protégé, Timothy: "I am mindful of the sincere faith within you, which first dwelt in your grandmother Lois and your mother Eunice, and I am sure that it is in you as well" (2 Timothy 1:5). The apostle recognized that this young man, whom Paul regarded as a son in the faith and fellow servant in ministry, was the product of a godly mother and grandmother.

How would you feel if your pastor said to you, "Your friends are following Christ just like you"? Can you think of a better compliment? Wouldn't you feel honored to hear some of your friends, neighbors, coworkers, and children remark that they are following Christ because of your example and influence?

You may argue, "I'm nothing special; my influence doesn't count for much." Don't sell yourself short. You are a woman in whom the Spirit of God resides. As you are energized by Him and then release that energy in service to your family and others, you make an impact. You may not see it right away, because the changes in others often happen gradually. But rest assured that your commitment to spiritual heart health will both inspire and motivate others around you to grow in their relationship with God.

Arlene, in her fifties, has such a ministry with her niece, Justine. In her wild and rebellious teen years, Justine got into drugs and sex—resulting in a child out of wedlock. After being clean and sober for a couple of years,

Justine fell back into her rebel behavior and recently gave birth to a second child by another father. But while she was pregnant, Justine was arrested for drug possession. She is currently undergoing detox in jail while her newborn son, addicted in the womb, is undergoing similar treatment at a children's hospital. Justine's first child is in foster care.

Arlene is heartbroken for Justine and her two babies. Arlene has spent many hours with her niece during the last two years, trying to encourage her and counsel her. Now she is helping Justine's mother—her sister-in-law—make important decisions about placement for the two children, who have been taken from Justine's custody. It's a tragic, real-life soap opera, but Arlene is making an impact through her prayers and service. She trusts that someday Justine and her two children will be drawn to Christ through her witness. In the meantime, she is content to love them and serve them in Christ's name with the energy He provides.

Your life may be markedly different from Arlene's, but you have just as many opportunities to be a conductor of God's energy for influencing others. Your husband, your children, your friends, your coworkers, your clients, your neighbors—they all need what you have. Tap into the spiritual energy God provides, and allow Him to duplicate His work in you in the lives of others you touch day by day.

Now we will talk about the energy-out side of energy balance for your physical heart, which focuses on consistent exercise. Our heart specialists have asked a fitness expert to supply this important chapter on exercise. As Kristy Brown talks about fitness in the next chapter, you'll want to zero in on her expert advice.

# Keys to Total Heart Health

## Chapter 15: Spiritual Energy for Every Hour of the Day

- For the spiritual heart, "energy in" focuses on a healthy spiritual "diet."

- Jesus expended tremendous amounts of energy daily, and He took in spiritual energy through communing with His Father, worshiping, and reading Scripture. If Jesus needed "energy in," how much more do we?

- The key to energy balance for Jesus was knowing how to replenish His energy, and it all starts with "energy in," receiving from God the fuel you need to nurture a strong spiritual heart.

- A simple outline for prayer at the beginning of the day is the acrostic SELF:

    Surrender your total self to God.

    Empty yourself of all the sin that would block the flow of His strength.

    Lift up praise to God.

    Fill yourself with the Holy Spirit by asking for His fullness.

- When it comes to dealing with obstacles and stresses in your life, prayer is your God-given "weapon of mass destruction."

- Strike a balance between times of quiet solitude and service to others, because if you use "spirituality" as an excuse to marginalize or ignore others, you are misusing the energy God has placed at your disposal.

- Tap into the spiritual energy God provides, and allow Him to duplicate His work in you in the lives of others you touch day by day.

## 16
## Heart Exercise
## for Fun and Personal Profit

Careful planning and variety are the keys
to your "energy-out" program.

**Kristy Brown**

Natalie, who works at a desk all day, has tried just about every diet out there, with little success. She stayed with each food program pretty well, but the pounds came off so slowly that she eventually lost interest and gave up. When her friends urged her to join a gym or buy a treadmill, Natalie argued, "I can't afford it. And besides, I hate exercising because I'm so uncoordinated."

Then Natalie's boss announced a challenge from the human resources department. Anyone in the office who would devote thirty minutes of his or her lunch hour to a brisk walk would be allowed to leave work a half hour early each day. A safe route around the outside of the building was proposed, with an alternative route designated inside the warehouse for bad-weather days. Her office promoted the exercise program to boost morale and reduce absenteeism.

Natalie loved the idea of leaving work early, and since she often just read a book during her lunch hour, she thought walking would be a good way to pass the time. So along with two dozen of her co-workers, Natalie brought a pair walking shoes to work and started walking each day at lunchtime.

The pace was a little fast for Natalie at first, and her feet hurt for a few days. But by the second week, she was keeping up with the pack and enjoying herself. She got acquainted with two girls in the office she barely knew, and as they walked and talked together each day, the time passed quickly.

The surprise to Natalie was that she began losing weight. She was on a modest diet at the time, trying to keep her calorie intake in check, but she had stalled short of her target weight—again. Now she was losing about one to two pounds a week. Delighted at seeing progress, she renewed her commitment to healthy eating habits and continued to shed pounds—and felt great doing it.

Natalie's story illustrates the importance of both sides of the energy-balance equation to Total Heart Health. Energy in—your caloric intake—is the single most dominant factor in controlling weight and preventing heart disease. But energy out—caloric output through physical activity and regular exercise—is equally important to good health and weight control. In this chapter, I will show you how to make your calorie-need profile work for your good health and weight control.

## Stay in Shape Like the Bible Says

You may ask, "If exercise is so important to physical heart health, why doesn't the Bible say something about it?" Well, the Bible does give us a general guideline for exercise in 1 Corinthians 6:19–20. We come back to this passage often when we talk about anything that can harm physical bodies and thus diminish or shorten our effectiveness to live for Christ in the world. Paul writes: "Didn't you realize that your body is a sacred place, the place of the Holy Spirit? Don't you see that you can't live however you please, squandering what God paid such a high price for? The physical part of you is not some piece of property belonging to the spiritual part of you. God owns the whole works. So let people see God in and through your body" (MSG).

The Bible doesn't specifically prohibit smoking or using harmful drugs. But we know these behaviors can seriously threaten our physical health and even kill us, so we stay away from them in our commitment to glorify God in His "temple"—our bodies. The same goes for eating too much, eating the wrong foods, or failing to get the exercise we need for proper health. Anything we do that endangers the body is disrespectful to God's temple and should be avoided.

But there's another very practical reason that the Bible doesn't specifically command us to participate in physical exercise. Most of those to whom the Bible was originally written didn't have a problem with fitness, because their lifestyle kept them fit. In biblical times, walking was the primary means of transportation. Furthermore, in a predominantly agrarian society, manual labor—farming, herding sheep, and the like—kept people physically active. They had few of the step-saving devices we enjoy today, so everyone logged plenty of steps every day.

Think about Jesus, for example. He was probably in excellent physical condition because He was even more active than most of His contemporaries. Growing up in a carpenter's home, He likely worked with Joseph into adulthood, which required chopping, sawing, and shaping wood. Once His ministry began, He spent three to four years crisscrossing the land of Palestine and beyond on foot, eager to preach, teach, and heal. He traveled between Judea in the south and Galilee in the north countless times, a journey of approximately eighty miles each way. His lifestyle kept Him fit.

Not so with twenty-first-century Americans. Most of us can get through the day without much movement at all. A car takes us everywhere we want to go. We ride the elevator instead of climbing the stairs, take our food off a supermarket shelf instead of growing and harvesting it or hunting for it, and cook by twisting dials on a range or pushing buttons on a microwave instead of gathering wood and building a fire. Many of us work by sitting at a computer all day, and much of the toil of manual labor has been eased by machinery. Unlike people in Jesus's day, most of us have to schedule our exercise outside of our work to keep ourselves fit.

## You're Different from a Man, and Your Exercise Should Be Too

Most people seem to feel that exercise should be the same for both men and women. For example, you may think that the men in Natalie's office who are dieting and walking every day as she is will lose the same amount of weight she does. In reality, there are a few significant differences between men and women that affect how they should exercise.

## Greater Amount of Exercise

As Drs. Duncan and Leachman mentioned earlier, women generally must exercise more than men to lose the same amount of weight. One reason is body fat, which women accumulate and store more readily than men. As women age, the ovaries produce less estrogen and androgens, and the body tends to store fat around the midsection.

## Increased Risk of Osteoporosis

Women also need exercise to prevent osteoporosis. Women are four times more likely than men to develop osteoporosis, a disease that makes bones more fragile and susceptible to fracture. Osteoporosis cannot be reversed, so prevention is vital. Exercise contributes to increased bone mass, especially in women who also take calcium supplements or hormone replacements.[1]

## Higher Commitment to Exercise

As mentioned previously in this book, women usually have different motives for exercise than men. Aside from better overall health, women tend to see exercise as a means to lose weight and improve their appearance. Men also work out to look "buff," but they are even more interested in exercise as a means to gain strength and speed. These differences mean that women sometimes need a higher commitment to exercise than men in order to achieve results. But when you make that commitment, you will experience a difference in total life quality!

# Your Complete Exercise Program

A complete exercise program consists of three categories of activity: cardiovascular, resistance, and flexibility. For the best results, combine all three based on your fitness needs. Cardiovascular exercises, the most important, are essential for keeping your heart strong and healthy. Resistance exercises help you with daily activities by developing strength for strenuous tasks such as lifting the kids in and out of car seats, pushing a wheelbarrow during gardening, or opening the tight lid on a new jar of pickles. Flexibility exercises will keep you mobile and limber with good range of motion throughout life. Let's look at each in detail.

## Cardiovascular Exercise for a Stronger Heart

Cardio exercise happens when you move your large muscle groups rhythmically and repetitively, such as in walking, running, biking, swimming laps, dancing, or stairstepping. Sustained, repetitive exercise elevates your heart rate, which facilitates blood flow, delivers oxygen to your cells, and increases metabolic rate. By taking advantage of her company's walk-at-noon plan, which is a cardiovascular workout, Natalie is off to a great start in developing an exercise regimen.

Even sex is good cardiovascular exercise. Experts estimate that sexual activity can be a significant calorie burner, though you should not assume that a normal, healthy sex life can replace other cardio exercises. And there is considerable evidence that people who exercise consistently have more energy and feel better about their appearance, which typically results in a healthier sex life. Cardio exercise and healthy sex are mutually beneficial.

Cardio exercise is always about progression—starting at a safe, comfortable level and periodically working up to realize greater benefits. Use the FITT scale to guide you as you progress in cardio exercise. *F* is for *frequency*, how many days a week you exercise. *I* is for *intensity*, the speed or energy level you put into your exercise. *T* means the *type* of exercise you do—walking, jogging, stepping, and so on. And *T* is for the amount of *time* you exercise each day. For example, Natalie exercises five times a week (frequency) for thirty minutes a day (time) by walking (type) at a steady, moderate pace (intensity).

In order to progress, increase your exercise by one FITT component at a time. For example, if you swim laps three mornings a week for forty-five minutes, consider lengthening your swim by five minutes every couple of weeks or adding a fourth morning. If you walk five days a week like Natalie does, you might try increasing the time from thirty minutes to forty minutes or the intensity from a moderate walk to a fast walk.

Always begin your cardio exercise with a four- to five-minute warmup and end with a three- to four-minute cool-down. For example, if you jog, warm up with some stretching and walking, and then end your jog by slowing your gait and walking. Warmup allows the heart rate to increase gradually, and cool-down brings it back to normal gradually, which is kinder to your heart.

## Resistance Exercise for Muscle Tone and Strength

Resistance exercises—also called strength training or weight training—use force on the muscles to strengthen them. Common resistance exercises are weightlifting, working out on resistance machines, and pressing against your own weight as in push-ups, pull-ups, and sit-ups. The American College of Sports Medicine recommends working all the major muscle groups. You have four muscle groups in your legs: gluteals, quadriceps, hamstrings, and calves. Your midsection contains two groups: abdominals and lower back. Exercises in this area are very important to good posture because these groups support your trunk and spine. There are five groups in your upper body: pectorals, upper back, shoulders, biceps, and triceps.

We recommend that you work each muscle group with one to three sets of eight to twelve repetitions—or reps—each. For example, eight consecutive push-ups or bench presses translate to one set of eight reps working the chest and triceps. After resting from this set, do another set of eight reps. Your goal should be to gradually increase your reps from eight to twelve and your sets from one or two to three. Develop other exercises to work the other muscle groups, such as squats for your legs and sit-ups for your midsection.

The level of difficulty for your resistance program can be measured on a continuum, moving from challenge to fatigue to failure. Start with a challenge and move to the point of fatigue. When you start out lifting weights, for example, select a weight that feels challenging. When a set of twelve lifts no longer fatigues you, it's time to add more weight. As your fitness level improves, you will be able to push yourself further before becoming fatigued. Over time, keep adding weights until, at the end of a set, you feel like you can't do one more lift—which is fatigue. Those who are more advanced push themselves past fatigue to the point of failure, meaning they keep lifting until they cannot physically complete a lift without the help of a trainer or spotter.

## Flexibility Exercise for Range of Motion

Flexibility, which is achieved primarily through stretching, is the most commonly neglected component of exercise. Many people ignore stretching because it doesn't seem to burn calories. But when you stretch properly, muscle fibers get longer. At age twenty, that may not seem like a big deal. But later in life, range of motion becomes crucial. People begin to notice their body tightening at about forty. Aching backs, for example, can often be alleviated with a few minutes of stretching each day. So no matter what your age, include stretching in your exercise plan to stay limber.

The American College of Sports Medicine recommends stretching all major muscle groups one to three times per workout session, one to three sessions a week. The best way to stretch is to extend the muscle and hold it there for ten to thirty seconds. You should feel tension but not pain. In reality, stretching can be the most relaxing part of your workout.

Some people stretch in the morning; others stretch before going to bed. Stretching is especially beneficial after a workout. Whenever you stretch, bear in mind that your muscles don't start on "ready." They need to be extended gently and stretched out gradually.

## Your Personal Exercise Routine

People usually exercise for one or two good reasons: to improve general health and/or to lose weight. No matter what your aim, our Total Heart Health recommendation is that at a minimum, you exercise for thirty minutes a day, five days per week. If you can't start at that level, at least make it your goal. Remember: if you are starting an exercise program for the first time, it is important to talk to your doctor first.

If general health is your goal, you can vary your exercise during the week. The minimum cardio exercise for general health is twenty minutes a day, three days a week. For example, you can walk for twenty minutes a day on Monday, Wednesday, and Friday, followed by ten minutes of core training (exercises for the abdominals and lower back) and stretching. Alternate this routine on Tuesday and Thursday with thirty minutes of resistance training.

In order to build more muscle, exercise a little more than thirty minutes a day, maintaining the three-day cardio and flexibility program while adding ten to fifteen minutes of resistance exercise before or after your cardio. On your two non-cardio days, do extended resistance exercises. To achieve muscle growth (hypertrophy), increase your weights and stay on the lower end of repetitions (eight to ten).

In order to lose weight, you must, of course, burn more calories than you take in with food. A minimum five-day, thirty-minute cardio exercise will help you burn calories. Initially you may do twenty to twenty-five minutes of daily cardio activity followed by five to ten minutes of stretching. But move up to a full thirty minutes of cardio as soon as possible and extend that time as your fitness improves. You can do the entire routine at one time or spread your exercise throughout the day. Just be sure to log at least thirty minutes daily. Once you reach that goal, work in at least another fifteen to twenty minutes of resistance exercise.

We recommend a maximum of one hour of strenuous exercise per day, six days a week. The Ten Commandments direct us to take a day of rest each week, and your body needs that rest. When you exercise, your body consumes glycogen, which is the sugar stored in the muscles. Observing an "exercise Sabbath" helps the muscles replenish glycogen stores.

Here's a sample exercise program based on thirty minutes of cardiovascular exercise each day. On days of longer exercise, it's all right to break your regimen into two sections, such as thirty minutes in the morning and thirty minutes later in the day. Always bookend each session with a few minutes of warmup and cool-down:

| | |
|---|---|
| **Monday** | 30 minutes of walking followed by stretching |
| **Tuesday** | 30 minutes on an elliptical trainer (step machine) |
| | 30 minutes of resistance exercise |
| **Wednesday** | 30 minutes of walking followed by stretching |
| **Thursday** | 30 minutes on a stationary bike |
| | 30 minutes of resistance exercise |
| **Friday** | 30 minutes on an elliptical trainer |
| **Saturday** | 30 minutes on a stationary bike |
| | 20 minutes of circuit training (alternating resistance exercises with two to four minutes of cardio movement, such as stepping, walking, cycling, or jumping rope) |

If you do not have access to a gym, fitness center, or in-home machines such as a treadmill or elliptical trainer, don't lose heart. You can still follow the program. Most people who don't work out at a gym use walking as their primary form of cardiovascular exercise. You can map out a challenging course or two in your neighborhood, perhaps including some hills. Or you may want to walk laps on the local high-school track or at an indoor mall.

There are cardio alternatives to walking, however. If you have access to a bicycle, use it. Just make sure you're pedaling consistently for the entire ride, because a simple cruise through the park doesn't count for much cardio. You are blessed if you live in an area where hiking trails, canoeing or kayaking, or cross-country skiing is readily available. These activities are great alternatives to walking. Enjoy them! Excercise videos are another great source for at-home workouts. There are hundreds of them on the market featuring every type of workout imaginable—from step aerobics to kickboxing to Pilates.

You don't need a gym for resistance exercise either. There are many low-cost exercise tools you can use right in your own home, such as dumbbells and exercise tubing. Here's a sample workout week using home-based devices for cardio and strength training.

| | |
|---|---|
| **Monday** | 30 minutes of walking, core training, and stretching |
| **Tuesday** | 30 minutes of walking or biking |
| | 30 minutes of resistance training using dumbbells or exercise tubing for squats, lunges, bicep curls, and crunches, as well as push-ups, pull-ups, etc. |
| **Wednesday** | 30 minutes of interval walking (meaning to alternate your pace between one minute of fast walking or jogging and two minutes at a more moderate pace) followed by core training and stretching |
| **Thursday** | 30 minutes of walking or cardio workout video |
| | 30 minutes of resistance training using dumbbells or exercise tubing |

| Friday | 30 minutes of walking, core training, and stretching |
|---|---|
| Saturday | 20 minutes of walking or biking |
| | 30 minutes of circuit training |

When you're ready for a more advanced workout, it might look like this:

| Monday | 45 minutes of an aerobic class followed by stretching |
|---|---|
| Tuesday | 30 minutes of fast walking plus 30 minutes lifting weights, targeting the upper body |
| Wednesday | 45 minutes on an elliptical trainer followed by stretching |
| Thursday | 30 minutes on a stationary bike plus 30 minutes lifting weights and circuit training, targeting the lower body |
| Friday | 45 minutes of kickboxing class followed by stretching |
| Saturday | 30 minutes of fast walking |

Find the program that works best for you, but don't be afraid to experiment. Exercise doesn't have to be difficult. Hold yourself accountable to others, such as those you walk with in the neighborhood or meet at the gym, to keep you on track. Try to think of your exercise time as an adventure and challenge instead of drudgery or duty. You can serve as your own personal trainer, but if you need more specific pointers for your regimen, consult a qualified fitness expert at a local gym.

Many women exercise while watching a talk show or news program on TV. Others slip on the headphones and listen to music. But your exercise time can be a great opportunity for prayer. One woman I know about talks to God while she walks or runs or bikes and listens to His still, small voice in the quietness of her heart. As exercise intensifies her focus, she says she seems to hear God more clearly.

As you embark on a new or accelerated personal exercise program, take heart. God designed your body to move, so regard exercise as a form of worship to Him. It is a specific way you can honor the temple of the Holy Spirit, your body. Paul urged, "Whether, then, you eat or drink or whatever you do, do all to the glory of God" (1 Corinthians 10:31). So exercise to the glory of God and present your body to Him as a "living and holy sacrifice" (Romans 12:1).

# Keys to Total Heart Health

## Chapter 16: Heart Exercise for Fun and Personal Profit

- Physically, there must be a balance between energy in and energy out. Energy in is your caloric intake, while energy out is your caloric output through physical activity and regular exercise.

- We must commit ourselves to glorify God in His "temple"— our bodies. Anything we do that endangers the body is disrespectful to God's temple and should be avoided.

- There are differences in the way women should exercise in contrast to men: women must exercise more than men to lose the same amount of weight; women need exercise to prevent osteoporosis; and women usually have different motives for exercise than men.

- A complete exercise program consists of three categories of activity: cardiovascular, resistance, and flexibility.

- Our Total Heart Health recommendation is that at a minimum, you exercise for thirty minutes a day, five days a week; and at a maximum, you strenuously exercise one hour per day, six days a week.

- The Ten Commandments direct us to take a day of rest each week. Your body needs that rest. Observing an "exercise Sabbath" helps the muscles replenish glycogen stores.

- Always bookend each session with a few minutes of warmup and cool-down.

- Physical Fitness Glossary

  - *Cardiovascular exercise*—Moving your large muscle groups rhythmically and repetitively, elevating the heart and breathing rates

  - *Resistance exercise*—Applying force to your muscles to strengthen them, as in weightlifting, resistance machines, tubes, or your own weight

  - *Flexibility exercise*—Improving your body's range of motion, primarily through stretching for 10 to 30 seconds per stretch

- *Core training*—Exercises that train the muscles of the center of the body—abdominals, lower back, and hips
- *Circuit training*—Alternating resistance exercises with two to four minutes of cardio movement, such as stepping, walking, cycling, or jumping rope
- *Elliptical trainer*—Exercise machines that move the feet in a circular motion, as in those that simulate running or stair climbing
- *Exercise tubing*—A rubber tube used for resistance training
- *Squats*—Exercises involving the upper legs, bending knees and hips (not more than 90 degrees) with body weight on the heels
- *Lunges*—Similar to squats, but working one leg at a time
- *Bicep curls*—Arms are down and extended, hlding weights, which are pulled up toward the shoulders by bending the arms
- *Crunches*—Abdominal exercises that flex the spine, placing the torso in a curved position

# 17
# Are You Getting
# Daily Spiritual Workouts?

A healthy spiritual heart needs exercise
as much as it needs fuel.

**Ed and Jo Beth Young**

As a young woman early in the twentieth century, Nan Eidsom was stricken with tuberculosis. In those days, contracting TB was tantamount to receiving a death sentence; so like many other victims of the disease, Nan was sent to a sanatorium to die.

But in God's providence, Nan got well. Deeply grateful to God for her recovery, she began taking care of other tuberculosis patients and chose healthcare as her profession. Eventually, Nan became director of the school of nursing at a large hospital, a position she held for almost half a century. She was known for her deep interest in both her nurses and the patients they served in the hospital.

But Nan Eidsom's heart for sharing Christ's love with people went far beyond her job description. She took needy people into her home and cared for them. And she couldn't keep new clothes in her closet because, whenever she met someone without enough to wear, she just gave her things away. Even into her eighties, Nan continued to walk the corridors at the hospital, though arthritis brought her pain with every step. Visiting in room after room, she demonstrated her Christlike concern through both her medical and her spiritual ministry to them. Having received so much from God, her lifelong pursuit was to give back to God through her skillful, compassionate service to others.

Nan, who was a friend of ours, is a wonderful example of spiritual energy balance. Having opened herself to God's grace and blessing in Christ, she generously poured herself out to others. She reminds us of Christ's words in Matthew 10:8: "Freely you received, freely give." Receiving from God, or taking in spiritual fuel from Him, is vital to spiritual heart health, just as eating healthy food is vital to physical heart health. But as Drs. Duncan and Leachman have so clearly outlined, diet—energy in—must be balanced by exercise—energy out, as Kristy Brown emphasized. Similarly, having freely received from God, we must freely give of ourselves to achieve healthy spiritual energy balance.

This doesn't mean your life will necessarily look like Nan's. Her loving ministry to others was the product of what God did in her and through her in light of her talents, abilities, gifts, personality, and passions. Your challenge is to funnel the energy you take in from God into service to Him and others that reflects how God made you.

## Work Out What God Works In

Do you realize that God has written a spiritual workout regimen right into His Word? Here it is: "Work out your salvation with fear and trembling; for it is God who is at work in you, both to will and to work for His good pleasure" (Philippians 2:12–13). The essence of our spiritual energy is the salvation God works in us. As we feed on Him, our heart grows strong. Why do we need a strong heart? Because God's plan is for us to direct that energy into serving others. We work out in service what God works into us through salvation. That's energy balance for the spiritual heart.

The Bible teaches us that salvation has three tenses: past, present, and future. Salvation past is called *justification*. Romans 5:1 says, "Therefore, having been justified by faith, we have peace with God through our Lord Jesus Christ." We believe that Jesus Christ is the Son of God and our only Savior and that we are sinners in need of salvation. Confessing and turning from our sin and receiving Christ, we are justified. It's a done deal, and from that moment our salvation is secured. Your justification means that as far as God the Judge is concerned, the words "Not Guilty" have been indelibly etched beside your name.

Salvation present is called *sanctification*. Paul wrote to the Thessalonian Christians, "Now may the God of peace Himself sanctify you entirely"

(1 Thessalonians 5:23). These people were already justified based on their past repentance and commitment to Christ. Paul now prays for their ongoing sanctification. To be sanctified means to be set apart for God's exclusive use. It's the process of being yielded to Him increasingly. We are being sanctified as we grow and mature in the Lord.

Salvation future is called *glorification*. At the end of time, when we see Christ face-to-face, even our bodies will be transformed into a quality like His (see Philippians 3:20–21). This will be the capstone to our salvation.

Salvation not only has three tenses, but it also impacts all three dimensions of our being. Justification happens in the spirit, where God "rescued us from the domain of darkness, and transferred us to the kingdom of His beloved Son" (Colossians 1:13). Sanctification occurs in the soul, as the salvation that awakened the spirit to God begins to transform our mind, will, and emotions. And glorification impacts the body, eventuating in our ultimate transformation into Christ's likeness.

But why did God justify us? And why does God continue to "work in" His salvation through sanctification? Is it only so that we can go to heaven when we die? That is certainly a wonderful part of it. But He has worked His salvation into us so we can work out our salvation in service to Him. Jesus said, "The Son of Man did not come to be served, but to serve, and to give His life a ransom for many" (Mark 10:45). If Christ's mission was selfless service, how can ours be anything else? We are not saved just to soak up as much of God and His Word as we can on our way to heaven. We are saved to serve in the energy He continually works into us.

Not only is God responsible for the salvation He works into us, but He is also the impetus behind our "workout" for Him. Paul goes on to say in Philippians 2:13, "It is God who is at work in you, both to will and to work for His good pleasure." Willing comes before doing. Thus God is at work in you to give you the will and to empower your work.

When the Bible says God is "at work" in you, it means He's doing something that cannot be frustrated or remain half-finished. If God is involved, you know the job will get done. Paul writes, "There has never been the slightest doubt in my mind that the God who started this great work in you would keep at it and bring it to a flourishing finish on the very day Christ Jesus appears" (Philippians

1:6 MSG). Once you give Him your life by making Christ your Lord, God starts working in you and through you and won't stop until He has finished the task!

So the Holy Spirit works into us the desire, the power, and the resources to do works pleasing to God. As we say yes to what He works into us, He releases the energy, the effective working of His power within us. Spiritual heart health results as we release and channel God's energy through our ministry to others.

## Your Spiritual Workout Routine

Sixteen-year-old Sally was the eldest of five children. Their father had passed away, and their mother was critically ill. Sally inherited the role of both father and mother to her four younger siblings. She cooked, got the kids off to school, cared for their mother, and served the family seven days a week.

One day, a self-righteous church member said to Sally, "I don't see you in church much."

"I'm just not able to attend as much as I would like to," Sally replied without further explanation.

"Then what are you going to tell God when you get to heaven about why you didn't go to church?" the woman pressed.

Sally answered, "I guess I'll just show Him my hands."

Sally is another shining example of working out what God has worked in. James described it this way: "If a brother or sister is without clothing and in need of daily food, and one of you says to them, 'Go in peace, be warmed and be filled,' and yet you do not give them what is necessary for their body, what use is that? Even so faith, if it has no works, is dead, being by itself" (James 2:15–17).

"Faith," in this passage, corresponds to spiritual energy in—our salvation. "Works" describes spiritual energy out—our service in Christ's name. Contrary to what much of the world assumes, good works won't save anybody. But contrary to what many Christians seem to believe, good works are a primary reason why we are saved. Paul links the two in Ephesians 2:8–9: "For by grace you have been saved through faith; and that not of yourselves, it is the gift of God; not as a result of works, so that no one may boast. For we are His workmanship, created in Christ Jesus for good works, which God prepared beforehand so that we would walk in them."

As Drs. Duncan and Leachman and Kristy Brown have reminded us, the person who eats and eats and eats but does no exercise whatsoever will get fat and flabby. In a similar way, the Christian who is always taking in—church services, Bible study meetings, sermon tapes, Christian books, and so on—and never giving out can become spiritually fat and flabby. Just as we must purposely plan plenty of physical exercise into our weekly routine to stay healthy, we must also purposely look for ways to work out our faith through selfless service to others.

Your loving service to others can be viewed as ministry in four concentric circles in your life. We challenge you to work out the salvation God has worked into your life beginning at home and spreading outward to your church, your community, and the world.

## Working Out at Home

You no doubt have a clear idea what "good works" means for you at home: it's the "work" that takes a "good" deal of your time. No matter what your family setting—single, married, kids, no kids, close extended family—there is always plenty to be done. Whether you have a job outside the home or not, your day-to-day chores likely include cooking, cleaning, laundry, childcare, yard work, and myriad other details that keep a family functioning.

If you're single, your workout at home may be the loving service and help you offer to parents, siblings, and extended family members. If you're married, you have a husband and perhaps children who will greatly benefit from your loving care. You may not consider the mundane business of housekeeping and parenting as spiritual exercise; it's just the stuff that somebody has to do and so you get it done. But it becomes a part of your spiritual workout at home when you view it from God's perspective. The Bible says, "Let every detail in your lives—words, actions, whatever—be done in the name of the Master, Jesus, thanking God the Father every step of the way" (Colossians 3:17 MSG). The key to spiritual exercise is in knowing for whom you are doing these tasks. For the Christian, nothing we have is really ours; it all belongs to God— including our homes and our family members. God has put these things under our care as stewards. So when you are taking your elderly parents to a doctor's appointment, you are transporting them for Jesus. The nightly ordeal of bathing the kids becomes the nightly ministry of bathing God's kids for Him. In reality, any job you do at home becomes an act of worship to God when you do it in His name.

In addition to the spiritual ministry of household tasks is the pointed spiritual ministry of sharing God and His Word with your family members. We see a beautiful template for this in the Old Testament. Moses commanded in Deuteronomy 6:6–9: "These words, which I am commanding you today, shall be on your heart. You shall teach them diligently to your sons and shall talk of them when you sit in your house and when you walk by the way and when you lie down and when you rise up. You shall bind them as a sign on your hand and they shall be as frontals on your forehead. You shall write them on the doorposts of your house and on your gates."

Christian education is the family's responsibility before it's the church's responsibility. More than anything you say, those around you are going to see God in how you live. Who God is and what God does and says also become transferable when it is part of the daily conversation in your home. Make it a point to share as wife and husband what God teaches you in your daily devotions, Bible studies, and sermons. Challenge your children to memorize Bible verses to recite and discuss at mealtimes—and offer prizes! When a child talks to you about a problem or a hurt, pray with him right on the spot so he learns that you include God in everything that concerns you. In short, anything you can do to keep God and His Word visible and approachable in your family is healthy spiritual exercise.

## Working Out at Church

Mrs. L. G. Gates was my (Edwin's) English teacher in junior high school in my hometown of Laurel, Mississippi. She taught me how to diagram sentences and recite poems like "The Rhyme of the Ancient Mariner." But the most important thing Mrs. Gates did for me as an eleven-year-old was to lead me to accept Jesus Christ as my Savior.

It happened at vacation Bible school one summer. I didn't really want to go, but my mother insisted. Besides, I heard about some of the activities that were planned and got excited about attending. VBS always concluded with a commencement ceremony in "big church." I was in line with the other kids when

Mrs. Gates suddenly called me away from the group. She talked to me about Jesus and led me in a prayer inviting Jesus into my life.

Some years ago, Jo Beth and I were visiting in Laurel, and someone told me that Mrs. Gates, then in her nineties, had slipped into a coma. I hadn't been home in a long time, but I told my friends and relatives, "I'm going to see Mrs. Gates. She may not know me, but she will hear me."

When I got to her bedside, I drew close to her ear and spoke her name. Then I quoted a few lines of poetry I remembered from junior high. I told her who I was and thanked her for what she had done for me. Then I quoted the words so dear to her—and to me: "For God so loved the world, that he gave his only begotten Son, that whosoever believeth in him should not perish, but have everlasting life" (John 3:16 KJV).

Thank God this dear saint found a place of ministry in our church. If she hadn't, perhaps I would not be writing this book today!

The church you attend is not just a "spiritual restaurant" where you go each week to get fed. If you only go to church to take in, you are missing out on at least 50 percent of the health benefit God has for you there. You are also called to exercise your faith in your church by ministering to others with the gifts, talents, and passion God supplies to you. Whether you serve in Sunday school or vacation Bible school, in the choir or praise band, on a church board or committee, in the drama ministry, on the visitation team, or on the cleanup committee, don't miss these vital fields of ministry available at your church.

## Working Out in the Community

The next circle for working out your faith is the community in which you live. A few years back, people in our church took the exercise of community ministry to a new dimension.

A tropical storm dumped torrents of rain on parts of Houston—mainly in areas where lower-income people lived. Flood damage was extreme. I visited one home where the mother was still in semishock. She walked us through the little house, showing where the water had crept up the walls. She took us into the living room and ran her hands along the mantel, demonstrating how she had clung to it to keep the waters from carrying her away.

In the aftermath, we decided to mobilize our church to aid flood victims.

Many of our people gave up their evenings and weekends, and during the day numbers of people were involved. They helped with cleanup, ripped out soggy carpet, repainted walls, and took on small carpentry tasks. In keeping with Colossians 3:17, our church's ministry to these people was performed in Christ's name.

America thrives on volunteerism. Every community has hospitals, PTAs, youth and children's organizations, homeless shelters, soup kitchens, orphanages, homes for battered women and unmarried mothers, and pregnancy centers. For the sake of the needy people in your community and for the sake of your spiritual health, find a place of service nearby and minister there with the energy God works into you! Jesus promises, "Whenever you did one of these things to someone overlooked or ignored, that was me—you did it to me" (Matthew 25:40 MSG).

## Working Out in the World

The whole world is full of need, so Jesus called us to share the gospel with the whole world. One woman we heard about is so enthusiastic about serving the world that she has dedicated an entire room in her home as her prayer center for the nations. A huge map of the world is mounted on one wall, and she prays across that map one nation at a time.

Another facet of your spiritual energy out should be focused on the church's mission to the world. Not all Christians are called to be overseas missionaries, but we are all called to be missionaries where we live and support the missionary work of others across the world. Pastor Rick Warren writes, "Telling others how they can have eternal life is the greatest thing you can do for them. . . . We have the greatest news in the world, and sharing it is the greatest kindness we can show to anyone."[1]

What about your job? God has placed you there as a missionary. For some of the people you work with, you are the only "pastor" they have. Be alert to their pains and crises, and be ready to minister to them. Start a prayer group or a Bible study before work or during lunch break. Make your work space a ministry center!

Even if you never travel outside your community to share the gospel, supporting the work of those who do is excellent spiritual exercise. Give generously to missions organizations that are taking the good news to the four corners of the world. Pray diligently for evangelists, missionaries, and their families by name. And whenever you have the opportunity, go in person, such as signing up for a short-term missions project.

You may be saying, "I just don't have the energy for exercise, either physical or spiritual. I'm doing well just to get to church on Sunday and read my Bible occasionally." You may lack the energy you need for ministry to others because you are skimping on your spiritual diet. As Italian poet Antonio Porchia observed, "A full heart has room for everything, and an empty heart has room for nothing."[2]

Make sure you are feeding regularly on God's Word. Be constant in prayer and worship. If you don't take in spiritual fuel, you'll quickly tire in your service to others. But if you are allowing God to work into your life His strength, you will have plenty of go-power for working it out in ministry.

# Keys to Total Heart Health

## Chapter 17: Are You Getting Daily Spiritual Workouts?

- To achieve healthy spiritual energy balance, having freely received from God, we must freely give of ourselves in service. Your challenge is to funnel the energy you take from God into service to Him and others that reflects how God made you.

- The essence of our spiritual energy is the salvation God works in us, then we work out in service to others what God works into us (see Philippians 2:12–13).

- Justification, God's forgiveness of our sins through Christ, happens in our spirits. Sanctification, being set apart and growing in the Holy Spirit's influence, occurs in our souls—our minds, wills, and emotions. Glorification is the transformation of our bodies at the end of time. Balance is allowing God to impact and change the total person.

- The person who eats and eats without exercising will get fat and flabby, and the same is true spiritually.

- We challenge you to work out the salvation God has worked into you in four concentric circles in your life—beginning at home and spreading outward to your church, your community, and the world.

- The key to spiritual exercise is knowing for whom you are doing your tasks. In reality, any job you do in these spheres is an act of worship to God.

- If you don't take in spiritual fuel, you'll quickly tire in your service to others. But if you are allowing God to work into your life His strength, you will have plenty of go-power for working it out in ministry.

## 18
# Be Your Own Diet Guru

Which of today's flashy pop diets
are best for you? None of them!

**Dr. Michael Duncan and Dr. Richard Leachman**

Callie's wake-up call came when her cholesterol count spiked dangerously high. The doctor had chided her before about the dangers of excess fat and cholesterol in her diet, but Callie just blew his warnings off. This time Dr. Jansen pulled out the gruesome photos of diseased hearts and coronary arteries and explained in detail what was happening to Callie's own organs. She returned home from the doctor's office and soberly announced to her sister, "I'm going on a diet."

Keisha's wake-up call came on her ninth anniversary. Every year, she and Derek celebrated by donning their wedding attire—including Keisha's beautiful and expensive gown—for an evening. Their two children especially looked forward to seeing mom in her gown and dad in his tux. Last year the gown was a tight squeeze for Keisha; this year getting it zipped was impossible. She was mortified. "This won't happen again next year," she promised Derek and the kids. "I'm dieting, starting tomorrow."

Marian's wake-up call came in the form of a passing remark from her grandson. After snuggling into her lap to read a book, little Brandon said, "Grandma, your belly is *huge!*" It wasn't a criticism or a judgment, because Brandon was only four years old. It was an innocently truthful observation on a par with his saying, "Grandma, the sky is purple today." But that day Marian made up her mind to lose twenty pounds.

Many people today, including heart doctors like us, have received heart health wake-up calls something like these. Whether it's the threat of a heart attack or a wardrobe that no longer fits, people realize they aren't eating right and decide to make changes. The big decision then involves what those changes look like. How much and how often shall I eat? Which diet is right for me?

There has been an evolution in thinking about diets in the United States during the past twenty-five to thirty years. As medical science began to learn more about the link between what we eat and our overall health, new dietary guidelines were published. And with each new wrinkle in dietary health came a new popular diet—or several new diets—telling the public what to eat and what to avoid. And large numbers of the population accepted these new approaches as gospel.

But as we have continued to learn more about food and health, diets that were once touted as the cure-all for heart problems and unwanted pounds seemed to go out of style like clothing fashions and hairstyles. Then another diet fad would spring up, and people flocked to the bookstores for the "answer" to their health and fitness needs. During the past few decades, it seemed as if there was a secret plot afoot in our country to devise an unending stream of new diets just to sell new books, diet foods, and exercise machines.

Marketing strategies aside, how do we know which diet is right for us? How can we sort through all the marketing hype to find an eating plan that goes beyond fashion, fad, and fiction to being both factual and fruitful in our pursuit of Total Heart Health?

In this chapter, we will answer these questions in two ways. First, we will look at a number of the kinds of diets that have evolved during the years and are still popular today in many forms. Second, we will review and crystallize the Total Heart Health approach to diet so you can evaluate and plan your personal heart health strategy.

## Eat No Evil

During the 1970s, the American Heart Association and most cardiologists told people to adhere to a diet low in saturated fat and cholesterol, assuring us that such a diet would lower the risk of blocked arteries and heart attacks. While this recommendation was logical and based on scientific evidence, the food and diet industry seemed to overreact. "Fat" and "cholesterol" became four-letter words, convincing the consuming public that all fat is bad.

As a result, the market was flooded with a seemingly unending variety of low-fat foods. This gave rise to a new problem. People began eating low-fat foods in great quantities as if they had nothing more to worry about. The focus of dietary strategy became *what* we eat instead of *how much* we eat. The subliminal message was, "As long as it's low in fat, you can eat as much as you want." But this approach compromised the benefits of the low-fat diet. It doesn't take a dietician to figure out that a double scoop of "50 percent less fat" ice cream does at least as much damage as one scoop of the regular stuff.

The other problem with the focus on fat was that it overlooked other elements posing a danger to heart health, such as excessive calories and carbohydrates. This was literally a fatal error, as evidenced by the clear statistical trend toward increased obesity in our country since the 1970s.

As the pendulum of thought swung back, carbohydrates became another big target of diets. The idea of decreasing carbohydrates in the diet was a logical one, since the low-fat message resulted in people's increasing their calorie intake from carbohydrates. For example, a meat-and-potatoes eater might cut back on roast beef to avoid fat and fill the void on her plate with another serving of mashed potatoes. The low-carb message went the other way: cut back on carbs—such as potatoes, pasta, breads, and sugar—and load up on protein, which meant meat and saturated fat. Again, there was no clear message from health authorities that total calories are the major issue in the diet.

A valid criticism among medical authorities of low-carb, high-protein, high-fat diets is that they are unbalanced. By eliminating or drastically reducing carbohydrates from the diet, an important food group is being ignored. This food group, in the form of fruits, vegetables, and whole-grain foods, contains many valuable nutrients essential to a healthy diet, specifically vitamins and minerals not present in a diet of high protein and fat.

The low-carb, high-protein diet has also been criticized as unhealthy because it may result in increased cholesterol values even as participants are losing weight. Another concern is the potential negative effect of a high-protein diet on kidney function.

Finally, an unbalanced diet, such as some of the fad diets targeting or eliminating food groups, is difficult to maintain long term. Any diet, even one based on a healthy balance of food groups, is a challenge of discipline over time. Further drastic restrictions only make it more difficult to establish and sustain a strict dietary lifestyle.

Each of these points is illustrated by a recent study that appeared in the *Journal of the American Medical Association* entitled "Comparison of the Atkins, Ornish, Weight Watchers, and Zone Diets for Weight Loss and Heart Disease Risk Reduction—a Randomized Trial."[1] At one year there was no difference in the amount of weight loss for those adhering to the low-carbohydrate diet (Atkins); the high-protein, low-glycemic diet (Zone); the very low-fat diet (Ornish); and the low-calorie/small portion size diet (Weight Watchers). Almost 50 percent of the participants in each diet dropped out of the study by twelve months, and for those who adhered to the diet, the weight loss was only ten to twelve pounds.

Losing weight and maintaining weight loss are difficult for most people. The best treatment for obesity and overweight is in prevention, by modest but persistent calorie restriction in conjunction with a regular exercise program and behavioral/spiritual modification as elucidated in the preceding chapters by Dr. Ed and Jo Beth Young.

So which of the fad diets is best for you? Probably none of them. We have a better idea.

## Eating with Balance

The Total Heart Health eating plan represents a balanced and reasonable approach to maintaining maximum health and a weight you can live with. The following is a focused summary of what we have been saying about diet in this book and is in line with the new 2005 Dietary Guidelines for Americans (prepared by the U.S. Department of Health and Human Services and the U.S. Department of Agriculture).[2]

### Calories

First and foremost, we recognize that total calorie consumption is the key to weight control. The average American consumes about 3,500 calories per day, which is twice the amount most people require to maintain normal body weight. Daily exercise is important and can help burn some of the excess calories. But even a full exercise program cannot fully compensate for a diet in which calories are out of control. We recommend a diet of 1,300 to 2,000 calories per day for most people, depending on the energy requirements of your lifestyle and activities, your gender, and your age.

## Carbohydrates

We generally agree with many diets that recommend reducing or eliminating simple sugars from the diet. We're talking about cutting back or cutting out all types of sugary soft drinks, cookies, cakes, sugar, potatoes, refined breads, and other foods with a high glycemic index. However, we encourage consumption of vegetables, fruits, and whole grains, which are lower on the glycemic index and contain valuable dietary components such as fiber, vitamins, and minerals.

## Protein

We recommend about one gram of protein per kilogram of ideal body weight. Your kilogram weight is your weight in pounds divided by 2.2. For example, if your ideal weight for your height is 150 pounds, you need about sixty-eight grams of protein per day. The problem is that most of us eat too much red meat for our protein needs, loading us up with high amounts of saturated fat. We recommend eating more fish and plant protein sources, which have fewer bad fats and contain other beneficial nutrients.

## Fats

We recommend eating fewer foods with saturated fats (animal fats, dairy products) and trans fats and increasing consumption of polyunsaturated fats, which are present in fish and vegetable oils (except tropical oils). Trans fats are especially difficult to eliminate because they are so prevalent in many of the foods we eat, such as fried foods, packaged foods, and baked goods. You will need to employ great diligence to recognize foods with trans fats and avoid them. Remember: the terms "hydrogenated" and "partially hydrogenated," sometimes seen on nutrition labels, are synonymous with "trans fat."

## Fiber

We recommend thirty-eight grams of fiber per day for adult men and twenty-five grams per day for adult women as a way to slow the digestive process and decrease the glycemic index of foods in the diet. Fiber assists in weight control by helping to curb hunger. Primary sources of fiber are whole grains and vegetables.

## Sodium and Potassium

We recommend a maximum of 2,300 milligrams (approximately one teaspoon of salt) of sodium per day. Individuals with high blood pressure, African-Americans, and older adults should try to consume no more than 1,500 milligrams of sodium per day, and should meet the potassium recommendation of 4,700 milligrams a day by consuming foods rich in potassium, such as fruits and vegetables. Like trans fats, salt can be found in many of the packaged foods we buy at the supermarket. It is wise to read the "Nutrition Facts" panel on food boxes and wrappers to help you avoid foods with high sodium content.

What will a menu plan based on these recommendations look like? In chapter 21, we have provided a three-week menu plan based on a target of approximately 1,300 calories per day. This plan is primarily designed to help overweight and obese persons lose weight through reduced calorie intake coupled with daily exercise. However, a 1,300-calorie diet may be too drastic a step for your lifestyle and health goals. So we recommend that you use this menu plan as a guideline for the varieties of healthy foods to include in your diet while tailoring the plan to suit you by increasing portion sizes and/or adding into the plan higher-calorie foods. As always, before embarking on a new diet plan, make an appointment to talk to your doctor about it.

There are just as many plans in circulation for your spiritual heart as there are diets for your physical heart. Dr. and Mrs. Young will help you sort through the advice of today's pop psychologists to discover what is helpful and harmful to Total Heart Health.

# Keys to Total Heart Health
## Chapter 18: Be Your Own Diet Guru

- The threat of a heart attack and a wardrobe that no longer fits are among the reasons people decide to change how they eat. They wonder how much and how often they should eat and which diet is right for them. Diets come and go like clothing fashions and hairstyles.

- Through the years, there has been an emphasis on lowering fats, then another on reducing carbohydrates. However, low-carb, high-protein, high-fat diets are unbalanced and difficult to maintain over the long term. Probably none of the fad diets are right for you.

- The Total Heart Health eating plan represents a balanced and reasonable approach to maintaining maximum health and a weight you can live with.

- We recognize that total calorie consumption is the key to weight control.

- We generally agree with many diets that recommend reducing or eliminating simple sugars from the diet.

- We recommend one gram of protein per kilogram of ideal body weight.

- We recommend fewer foods with saturated fats and trans fats, and increased consumption of polyunsaturated fats.

- We recommend twenty to thirty grams of fiber per day.

- We recommend a maximum of 1,500 milligrams of sodium per day.

- As always, before embarking on a new diet plan, ask your doctor about it.

# 19
# Get Your Guidance
# from the Guardian of Your Heart

Which of today's pop psychologists
should you follow? None of them!

**Ed and Jo Beth Young**

Would you like to know the path to a healthy heart and soul? One very popular authority on the subject recommends that you make a "life map" in order to discover what you want for yourself and your life. Here's how you do it.

Gather a stack of magazines and catalogs and a large piece of poster board. Leaf through the publications and cut out any words, phrases, or pictures that seem to speak to you in some way or evoke your feelings. Place all your cutouts on the poster board, then arrange and adjust them until they feel just right to you. Once you are pleased with the arrangement, glue your collage onto the board.

When your life map is finished, study it and ask yourself these questions: "What have I learned about myself by looking at my life map? Do I see any patterns? Does anything on my life map surprise me? If I knew that all the images on my life map would become real in my life, would I be okay with it? Who do I need to become in order to fulfill the intentions of my life map? Based on my life map, what quality will I commit myself to develop this year?"

At some point, you will want to share your feelings and discoveries with a friend and create life maps together. This authority suggests that you are responsible for your own life, so you must take control and run your own life. That's what she has been doing, and millions of women are following her advice.

Just like physical health, spiritual health is big business today. People are even more desperate for peace of mind and fulfilling relationships than they are for a healthy, fit, attractive body. That's why the self-help, pop philosophy, pop psychology, and New Thought sections at the bookstore are even bigger than the health and fitness sections. That's also why people like Oprah Winfrey, Dr. Phil McGraw, and other self-help personalities attract such a huge following. People are soul-sick, heartbroken, lonely, and depressed, and they will listen to anyone who offers good-sounding advice for healing the painful crises of the heart and soul.

Whose books should we buy and read? Which TV psychologist or pop philosopher should we listen to? Which of the many women's magazines in the grocery-store checkout line will steer you straight regarding solving problems of the heart?

## God or the Gurus?

We can't say it more plainly than this: the foundation for spiritual heart health is God and His Word. We're talking about the God who created your soul and spirit as well as your body. He knows all about the struggles and pain of the human heart. The personalities, celebrities, and authorities you must look to first for spiritual heart health are those who are 100 percent committed to what God has to say about the heart. The books, magazines, and tapes you should consult first are those whose content is based on the Bible.

Apart from this foundation, we are left with the best thinking and reasoning humankind can offer. By God's design, human intellect is a marvelous tool. But our knowledge and perspective are so limited compared to what God knows and sees. Ephesians 4:17–18 describes people who walk in the "futility of their mind, being darkened in their understanding." Colossians 2:8 speaks of the "philosophy and empty deception . . . the tradition of men . . . the elementary principles of the world." You don't want to base the health of your spiritual heart on counsel drawn from futile, darkened, empty minds without God. You need God's perfect Word, not humanity's best guess.

Oprah Winfrey is the queen of today's pop culture. *Fortune* described her as the "therapist for an anxious nation."[1] Indeed, she has done much to inspire, challenge, and encourage people around the world, and her programs are frequently helpful and uplifting. You just need to be aware that her foundation for spiritual and emotional counsel is *self*, not *God*. The Bible says, "The fear of the LORD is the beginning of wisdom, and the knowledge of the Holy One is understanding" (Proverbs 9:10). Who are you going to trust as your source of wisdom and understanding: yourself or God?

Dr. Phil McGraw, the self-styled "life strategist," was launched to national prominence as a frequent guest on Oprah's television program. Dr. Phil has also contributed much good to viewers through his commonsense, easy-to-understand advice. But for many of his disciples, Dr. Phil's "Ten Life Laws" supplant the Ten Commandments as a prescription for living. Again, the focus is on self instead of God.

Marianne Williamson is another self-focused guru of self-help and self-realization. She is author of *A Course in Miracles* and pastor of Church of Today, a Unity congregation in suburban Detroit described as "one of the largest and fastest growing New Thought churches in the United States." Women, Wilson writes in *A Woman's Worth,* are called to be "goddesses."[2]

Deepak Chopra is positioned as a world-class authority on the human heart. *Forbes* magazine called Chopra "the latest in a line of gurus who have prospered by blending pop science, pop psychology, and pop Hinduism."[3] Self-knowledge, Chopra believes, can transform the world. "I want a day to come," he writes, "when the study of self-knowledge becomes an integral part of the educational system," because that could lead to "a world of peace, harmony, laughter and love."[4]

Gary Zukav wrote *The Seat of the Soul* and spawned a national movement of "Soul Circles," where people gather to discuss his ideas. For Zukav, the soul is working across time through reincarnation to become a "multisensory being."[5] The soul itself is a creator of sorts, and the "personality emerges as a natural force from the soul."[6]

Iyanla Vanzant is a priestess of the Yoruba religion. There is a "Valley of Light," she writes, that people can experience when they get with themselves. To do that, "a woman must be willing to translate being 'by yourself' to being 'with yourself.'" She says, "When you are with yourself, you receive the blessing of enlightenment."[7]

These gurus and many others like them have different ways of expressing their principles, laws, notions, concepts, and ideas, but they all have the same focus: self. This preoccupation is as old as the Garden of Eden. Eve's "guru" was the serpent. Eating the forbidden fruit, Satan promised, would make her a goddess. She succumbed to the temptation to displace the real God from the throne of her life and elevate herself to that position. And humankind has suffered from spiritual heart disease ever since.

Putting self on the throne where God belongs is not the cure to the soul's ailments; rather, it is the central cause of spiritual heart disease. G. K. Chesterton, twentieth-century Christian journalist and author, was asked in an article by an editor of the *London Times*, "What is wrong today with the world?" Chesterton is said to have written back, "Dear Sir, in response to your question, 'What is wrong with the world?' I am."[8]

## The Guardian of Your Heart

Any pop psychologist who elevates the human spirit above the Holy Spirit is detracting from, not contributing to, your spiritual heart health. You can only find reliable help and advice in those who direct you back to "the Shepherd and Guardian of your souls" (1 Peter 2:25). Why should you seek Christ's counsel and healing for your heart? We can think of several reasons.

### Jesus Knows You Better Than Anyone

As much as the self-help gurus appear to understand the inner self, none of them can claim to have created you and your heart. Nothing exists that wasn't created through Jesus, writes His disciple John (John 1:3). That means you, everything about you, inside and out, physical and spiritual. John also notes that Jesus needed no one to teach Him about human nature, because "He Himself knew what was in man" (John 2:25).

The real issue behind any world-view is its authority. When the lifestyle gurus of the world expound their theories, it is reasonable to question the authority on which their claims are based. Pop psychology rests on the subjective authority of its various gurus. But the Creator of the universe and of your heart offers objective truth based on His intricate knowledge of you.

## Jesus Speaks the Truth About Your Heart

Sin is at the core of all spiritual heart problems. Yet none of the pop soul doctors preach, "All have sinned and fall short of the glory of God" (Romans 3:23). Rather, they talk about the great enlightenment that can come from the self (Vanzant), the potential of self (Chopra), and the authentic self (Dr. Phil). They never speak of the sinful self. In fact, Marianne Williamson's *A Course in Miracles* holds that sin is an illusion.

Failing to deal with sin in the human heart is a hindrance, not a help, to spiritual heart health. Jesus tells you the truth about your heart's problems and then offers you His lifesaving remedy: Himself.

Many helpful resources are available that will fortify your heart and help you discern the truth about life and relationships. Fill your mind with good life-coaching material based on biblical principles. Listen to Bible teaching tapes. Invite a wise, mature, trusted Christian friend to serve as your mentor and sounding board. The Bible is the ground of truth about what your heart needs, but there are many avenues through which God's Word is taught.

## Jesus Sets You Free from Self-Focus So You Can Focus on Others

Self-focus, as preached in pop psychology, is a stifling prison. Egomania is the disease that results. Developmental psychologist Erik Erikson wrote about the "stagnation" of self-absorption that afflicts some people late in life. They lose "generativity," the ability to look beyond themselves to the needs of others. The self-focus that is the core of pop psychology is not healthy.

Jesus struck a healthy balance between self-focus and others-focus. Love your neighbor as you love yourself, He said (see Luke 10:27). He called it the second greatest commandment. But to fulfill this commandment, we must also fulfill the first: love God with all your heart, soul, strength, and mind. Proper equilibrium between self-love and other-love is achieved only as we place God-love first. By loving God supremely, we are liberated from the worship of self, which is deadly idolatry. Healthy self-love results when we put God at center stage in our hearts. In so doing He gives us a right perspective of love, and we begin to love others above ourselves just as Jesus loves us.

## Jesus Doesn't Deny Your Guilt; He Removes It

For many of the pop psychologists, there is no objective personal guilt, only an illusion of wrongness. The spirituality represented by these self-help gurus is an "unremarkable New Age hodgepodge," says Amy Welborn, and is "not about sin, redemption, sacrifice, conversion, humility, holiness and Jesus Christ."[9]

Jesus lays out the real problem and the real solution. We have sinned and broken God's law, and the resulting objective guilt is eternal and absolute. Our only hope for heart healing is to face our guilt by confessing our sin and receiving His innocence. When we do, Romans: 8:1–4 promises,

> There is now no condemnation for those who are in Christ Jesus. For the law of the Spirit of life in Christ Jesus has set you free from the law of sin and of death. For what the Law could not do, weak as it was through the flesh, God did: sending His own Son in the likeness of sinful flesh and as an offering for sin, He condemned sin in the flesh, so that the requirement of the Law might be fulfilled in us, who do not walk according to the flesh but according to the Spirit.

The gurus don't want to talk about guilt because they can't remove it. To raise the issue brings into focus an insurmountable problem no amount of books, chatter, tapes, or rallies can overcome. All these gurus can offer you is empty philosophy, futile thinking, and deception. But Jesus Christ gives you the truth that sets your heart free!

We're not saying that you should never watch Oprah, Dr. Phil, or other pop psychologists and counselors on TV. There is some entertainment value in these programs, and occasionally you may learn something helpful, because even people who don't hold to the Bible can stumble upon biblical truth. But when you watch, do so with your Bible open—meaning, sift their principles and advice through the truth of the Word of God. If one of them offers advice that *sounds* right, check it against Scripture to make sure it *is* right before you accept it or recommend it to others.

The journey to Total Heart Health is a lifelong, disciplined pursuit. As you embark upon it, we trust that you won't journey alone. If you are single, ask a trusted friend to journey with you. Consider sharing your insights and goals with an important man in your life: brother, father, adult son, fiancé. If you are married, we trust that your husband will be a soul mate not only for your life but for your heart health.

We have prepared a message especially for the most important men in your life. If possible, encourage your husband, boyfriend, father, or brother to read the next chapter, and invite him to be your cheerleader.

# Keys to Total Heart Health

## Chapter 19: Get Your Guidance from the Guardian of Your Heart

- Just like physical health, spiritual health is big business today. People are even more desperate for peace of mind and fulfilling relationships than they are for a healthy, fit, attractive body.

- We can't say it more plainly than this: the foundation for spiritual health is God and His Word. The personalities, celebrities, and authorities you must look to first for spiritual heart health are those 100 percent committed to what God has to say about the heart.

- Any pop psychologist who elevates the human spirit above the Holy Spirit is detracting from, not contributing to, your spiritual heart health.

- Sin is at the core of all spiritual heart problems. Today's pop gurus don't preach that "all have sinned" (Romans 3:23), but rather that self is a source of healing.

- Self-focus, as preached in pop psychology, is a stifling prison, and Jesus sets you free from its misery so you can find the joy of focusing on others.

- For many of the gurus, there is no objective personal guilt. Jesus doesn't deny your guilt; He removes it.

- If you watch the gurus, sift their principles and advice through the Word of God.

## 20
# Are You Ready
# for the 90-Day Challenge?

Is "next Monday" a good time for you
to start transforming your life?

**Ed and Jo Beth Young**

For years, we've had a running joke around our house. It has gotten to the point that all Edwin and I need to say to provoke a good laugh is, "I'm starting Monday." Here's how it happened.

Sometimes while watching TV or leafing through a women's magazine, I discover a new plan for healthier living—a fad diet or menu plan, a miracle pill, or a new workout regimen. When I relate my exciting discovery to Edwin, he will say something like, "That's great, Jo Beth. When are you going to start?" I respond resolutely, "I'm starting Monday." The first day of the workweek always seems like the perfect time to change my life.

Well, "Monday" rarely comes. The more I look forward to it, the more the restrictions of a new plan seem dull and boring. So I often will talk myself into putting off the new plan a day or two. Or, if I do make it through a Monday or several days or even a week or two, my ardor soon cools and the new plan is shelved. So whenever Edwin says to me, "How's your new plan going, Jo Beth?" my stock answer has been, "I'm starting *next* Monday." We've enjoyed a lot of good laughs over that line.

But after Edwin's scary heart incident, we were both highly motivated for one more "next Monday." We didn't begin a new fad plan to lose a few pounds; we launched into a new lifestyle of Total Heart Health, a lifestyle we have maintained for more than fifteen years.

What about you? You have finished the book, having perhaps highlighted or underlined many passages you want to remember and put into practice. When will you take the vital step from *wanting* to change and *knowing* you must change to *initiating* a life-changing transformation? The first day of the work-week really is a great time to begin a lifestyle of Total Heart Health. And the day you take up the 90-Day Challenge you will begin a life-changing process. Does Monday work for you?

In the introduction, I invited you to consider making a Lifestyle Transformation Commitment. If you haven't done so already, now is the time to go back to the form on page xiii, and set your Total Heart Health transformation in motion. Fill in the blanks and prayerfully sign your name. Select a starting date, plan your menus, and map out your physical and spiritual fitness plan. Then go for it! I underscore what I promised at the front of this book: three months from now, if you faithfully follow the Total Heart Health plan, you will look into the mirror and see a new woman, healthier in spirit and body!

## Change Is a Process

Whenever I (Edwin) make a decision to change my spiritual, dietary, or fitness habits, I often wish I could wake up the next morning and be completely transformed. But any kind of significant change in our lives is a process of five stages: precontemplation, contemplation, preparation, action, and maintenance.[1] In other words, before we can think about a change, we have to *think about thinking about it*. Before we take some steps, we have to make our plans. And once we make some changes, we have to maintain the new lifestyle.

The fact that you have taken time to read this book indicates that you've passed the first two stages. You're ready to make some plans and start moving forward on your 90-day track to a Total Heart Health lifestyle.

Most models of behavioral change focus on feelings, thoughts, and behavior. They often don't succeed because they ignore the fundamental power of change, which is spiritual. In this book we have detailed a simple program for enriching your relationship with God, which is where all health begins.

However, you can have the loftiest goals for change and the best plans to get you there, but if you don't make the decision to change and follow through, transformation won't occur.

## Journaling Your 90-Day Challenge

In this chapter we want to give you another tool to help you start and maintain the 90-Day Challenge. We call it the Total Heart Health Journal. You'll find sample sheets on pages 208–10.[2] Feel free to photocopy these pages or simply hand-copy the headings into the journal you already use. At the conclusion of the 90-Day Challenge, you may continue to use these pages to maintain the lifestyle you have adopted.

For each day, begin by writing in the day of the challenge (such as Day 1, Day 26, and so on), the date, or both. The headings on each journal page will help you keep track of the four key elements for the Total Heart Health lifestyle we have discussed in this book: spiritual energy in, physical energy in, spiritual energy out, and physical energy out. You may want to keep your journal with you and make entries throughout the day. Or it may work better for you to sit down with your journal at the end of the day and make the appropriate entries. Whatever method you choose, using this journal template will help you stay on track day by day.

Look upon this template as a guide offering direction and encouragement instead of a law requiring obedience. Few things are less inspiring than a hard, cold directive that demands, "Do this or else!" Rather, make the Total Heart Health Journal work for you. Use only the sections that encourage you in the right direction. Allow this experience to assist you in the direction you want to go.

### Spiritual Energy In

The first section will encourage you toward a strong spiritual heart. We recommend that you spend about thirty minutes a day reading from the Bible and connecting with God in prayer. Enter the reference to the Bible passage you read in the space provided. You may want to take a book of the Bible—such as

Genesis, John, Romans, or Proverbs—and read one chapter each day. You may want to skip around the Bible, reading from a different section each day—Old Testament, New Testament, Gospel, epistle, poetry, history. If you don't know where to start reading in the Bible, consider using the ninety passages provided in chapter 22, which will take you through your 90-Day Challenge.[3]

As you read, ponder the two questions on the blank journal sheet to help you summarize what you get out of your daily reading. This is your chance to respond to what God says to you in the Bible each day. Jot down what you sense He is telling you and how you want to respond. There are no right or wrong answers here. God speaks to our hearts through His Word, so you will tap into His heart as you read. Simply summarize what you find and identify what you sense He is asking you to do.

The next section is prayer. We suggest that you use your thumb and four fingers to help you remember specific things you want to pray about. Jot down in the space provided what you pray for. When God answers that prayer in some way, write down the answer and the date. Keeping a record of answered prayer will encourage your faith and strengthen your prayer resolve.

*Thumb.* The thumb stands for thankfulness, just like a thumbs-up stands for "Everything's great." A grateful heart is a healthy heart emotionally and mentally. Gratitude keeps moving us forward because it reminds us of the blessings of the past. It's good to start your personal prayer time with thanks and praise.

*Index finger.* Your index finger is your "pointer," which we commonly use to give or confirm directions. So your pointer finger prompts you to seek God for His direction, guidance, and right decisions. Ask God each day for His direction for your life in general and specifically in the tasks and experiences you will face.

*Middle finger.* Our middle fingers are usually the tallest, reminding us to pray for those who "stand tall" in authority over us. Pray for God's provision and blessing on city, county, state, and national leaders. Pray for your pastor and other church leaders. If you work outside the home, pray for the managers in your workplace. Pray for these people by name whenever possible.

*Ring finger.* The ring finger represents those within your closest circle of love: your husband, children, parents, grandchildren, extended family members, and closest friends. The ring finger also reminds us of commitment.

Whenever you say to someone, "I'll pray for you," you're making a commitment. Write the names of these people under this heading and fulfill your commitment to pray for them.

*Pinky.* Finally, your little finger or pinky symbolizes people in society who are downtrodden, neglected, defenseless, and poor. There is a special place in God's heart for the impoverished—widows, orphans, single moms, the homeless, those unable to hold productive jobs because of health issues. Pray for organizations and ministries that work to alleviate human suffering in some way.

Praying for people is a motivator to actively express love for others, especially those in need around you. James says it is not enough simply to say to a hungry person, "Be full!" (see James 2:14–17). Praying for the down and out should prompt loving, sacrificial action to lift them up and pull them in.

## Physical Energy In

Dr. Mike Duncan and Dr. Rick Leachman have provided a treasure of information in this book, equipping you to implement a daily menu that is nutritious and delicious. You may choose to track your daily calorie intake in this section based on your individual calorie-need profile. You may also find it helpful to jot down what you eat each day: foods, portions, water intake, vitamins, and so on. If you decide to follow the weight-loss menu plan in chapter 21, you can summarize how you're doing here.

## Spiritual Energy Out

This could be the most exciting section in your daily journal. How is God using you each day to serve the needs of others—at home, at church, in your community, in the world at large? In what ways are you working out what God has worked in your life? Were you able to help someone in distress today? Were you able to share your faith in Christ with someone who is not a Christian? Did God prompt you to stop and pray with or encourage someone today—a coworker, a family member, even a total stranger? Did God use you to brighten someone's day, lighten their load, or point them to Jesus? As you keep track of these "divine encounters" in your journal, they will keep you alert to the needs of others throughout your daily activities, allowing you to grow stronger "muscles" of faith and service.

## Physical Energy Out

In chapter 16, Kristy Brown gave you valuable information to help you put together a daily exercise plan that's just right for you. She recommends a minimum of thirty minutes a day of moderate exercise six days a week. This section of your journal will guide you in recording how well you do each day at staying with the regimen you have decided to follow.

## A Total Heart Health Lifestyle

What happens at the end of your 90-Day Challenge? Commencement. When we were in school, we thought commencement meant "the end," didn't we? No more classes, textbooks, or homework. But we now know that the word *commencement* means the beginning, not the end. When you graduated from high school or college, you *commenced* a productive life in your chosen field. In the same way, the last day of your 90-Day Challenge is your commencement into a fulfilling, rewarding, and satisfying lifestyle of Total Heart Health. Jo Beth and I have stayed with the program for more than fifteen years, so we know you can do it!

We could leave you with any number of worn-out motivational clichés: "The journey of a thousand miles begins with a single step"; "If it is to be, it is up to me"; "Today is the first day of the rest of your life." But we believe that the promise and potential of a Total Heart Health lifestyle is no better summarized than in these words from the apostle Paul. This is our heartfelt prayer and hope for you.

May God himself,
the God who makes everything holy and whole,
make you holy and whole,
put you together—spirit, soul, and body—
and keep you fit for the coming of our Master, Jesus Christ.
(1 Thessalonians 5:23 MSG)

# Keys to Total Heart Health

## Chapter 20: Are You Ready for the 90-Day Challenge?

- When will you take the vital step from *wanting* to change and *knowing* you must change to *initiating* a life-changing transformation?

- To begin, select a starting date, plan your menus, and map out your physical and spiritual fitness plan.

- Most models of behavioral change focus on feelings, thoughts, and behavior. They often don't succeed because they ignore the fundamental power of change, which is spiritual. Your relationship with God is where all health begins.

- The Total Heart Health Journal, included here, will help you get started on the 90-Day Challenge. For a more detailed plan of action, get *The Total Heart Health for Women Workbook* (Thomas Nelson, 2005).

- We recommend you spend about thirty minutes a day reading from the Bible and connecting with God in prayer. A helpful tool is *Daily Strength for Total Heart Health* (Countryman, 2005).

- Summarize in your journal what you get from your daily reading.

- Journal your daily physical diet and exercise, along with energy-out activities in service to others.

- Our heartfelt prayer and hope for you is this: "May God Himself, the God who makes everything holy and whole, make you holy and whole, put you together—spirit, soul, and body—and keep you fit for the coming of our Master, Jesus Christ" (1 Thessalonians 5:23 MSG).

# Total Heart Health Journal

## Day_____

### SPIRITUAL ENERGY IN

**Today's Bible Passage** _____

What do you sense God is saying to you in the passage you read?

How will you respond to God's message to you today?

### Today's "Hand" Prayer

*Thumb:* Tell God what you are thankful for.

*Index Finger:* Pray for God's direction in your life and in the lives of others.

*Middle Finger:* Pray for those in authority in your church, country, workplace, and so on.

*Ring Finger:* Pray for your spouse, children, family members, close friends, and so on.

*Pinky:* Pray for the poor, neglected, oppressed, and abused.

### PHYSICAL ENERGY IN

Note your food intake today under the headings you want to track:

Approximately how many calories did you take in today?

What did you eat today?

Breakfast

Lunch

Dinner

Snacks

What was your water intake today (six twelve-ounce glasses recommended)?

Did you take your vitamins/supplements/medications today?

## SPIRITUAL ENERGY OUT

In what ways did you exercise your faith today in loving service to others?

In your home:

In your church:

In your community:

In the world:

## PHYSICAL ENERGY OUT

Note the exercise you accomplished today under the headings you want to track.

Total time spent exercising (minimum of thirty minutes recommended):

Type and time of cardiovascular exercise:

Type and time of resistance (strength) exercise:

Type and time of flexibility (stretching) exercise:

Did you allow time for warmup and cool-down?

What is your weight today?

*Photocoopy these sample pages for your own Total Heart Health Journal.*

# 21
# Physical Energy In: Menus and Recipes

Twenty-one days of easy, healthy weight-loss menus for you and your family.

The menus we share with you capture the wholesome goodness of common foods in delicious, easy-to-prepare meals in portions that will help you lose weight. These meals are rich in fruits, vegetables, and whole grains, making them high in fiber and low in saturated fats and trans fats. Each daily menu averages approximately 1,300 calories. If your dietary plan requires more calories, you may increase the serving sizes or include foods that up the calorie count. Be sure to talk to your doctor before starting this or any other diet plan.

The following table breaks down the daily average distribution of metabolic fuels and other important nutrients.

## Total Heart Health Menus
## Nutrition Summary
## Daily Average 1,300 Calories

| | | |
|---|---|---|
| Protein | 92 grams | 28 percent of calories |
| Carbohydrates | 155 grams | 46 percent of calories |
| Fats | 40 grams | 26 percent of calories |
| Fiber | 25 grams | |
| Sodium | 2,500 mg | |
| Potassium | 2,600 mg | |

As with all low-calorie diets, however, the Total Heart Health menus may not fulfill all the recommended portions of nutrients according to the National Academies of Sciences. So we recommend that any adult who adopts this eating plan supplement his or her diet with one multivitamin and 600 mg of calcium daily.

These menus provide the weekly amount of omega-3 fatty acids recommended by the American Heart Association by including seafood at least twice a week.[1] However, persons with chronic illnesses such as heart disease and autoimmune disorders should receive 1,000 mg of omega-3 fatty acids per day, which usually requires three to five capsules of fish oil supplement daily.

It should be noted that not all condiments used in these menus are fat free, notably the salad dressings. We caution you not to use all fat-free condiments when the meal itself is generally low in fat, because nutrient absorption will be negatively affected. A recent study in the *American Journal of Clinical Nutrition* revealed that substantially greater absorption of carotenoids (lycopene, alpha and beta carotene) was observed when salads were consumed with full-fat rather than reduced-fat salad dressing.

These menus and recipes are relatively low in sodium. If salt or salty foods, such as bouillon, are added in the food preparation, daily sodium intake will be higher.

## General Menu Guidelines

As you use the weight-loss menus we provide, here are some important guidelines to keep in mind.

*Servings.* Unless otherwise noted, these menus are presented in servings for one person. If others in your household are following this plan, simply add additional servings for them.

*Eggs.* Eggs are a good source of protein and are included in several breakfast menus. But eggs should be prepared without fat, such as boiled, poached, or fried in fat-free cooking spray. We recommend that you use omega-3 enriched eggs whenever possible, such as Eggland's Best, EggsPlus, on Christopher Eggs.

*Bread and cereal products.* Whenever this menu calls for bread, toast, crackers, dinner rolls, and the like, we recommend 100 percent whole-grain products, which provide at least three grams of fiber per serving. As for breakfast cereals, buy low-fat, whole-grain hot and cold cereals that contain at least four grams of fiber per serving.

*Sweeteners.* If you wish to sweeten menu items such as dry or cooked cereal, we recommend a calorie-free sugar substitute. But stay informed about possible side effects from non-nutritive sweeteners.

*Spreads.* If you wish to add a buttery spread to bread or cooked vegetables, we recommend a butter substitute, such as imitation butter flakes.

*Fresh fruit.* Whenever a menu calls for "1 fresh fruit," you may use one of the following: one medium orange, apple, peach, nectarine, or pear; one-half grapefruit; one-half cantaloupe; one cup melon chunks; two small plums or kiwis; one cup strawberries; one-half cup other berries (blueberries, raspberries, blackberries); one small banana; one cup grapes (freeze them for fun!); or one-half cup fresh pineapple or canned pineapple in its own juice.

*Raw vegetables.* Whenever a menu suggests a snack of raw veggies, one serving is filled with either two stalks of celery, six baby carrots, one medium green pepper, one medium tomato, or other vegetables in equivalent amounts.

*Fish.* Whenever a menu entrée features fish, we recommend red snapper, sole, tilapia, flounder, albacore, or salmon. Whenever possible, use cold-water fish instead of farm raised.

*Beverages.* No beverages are included in these menus or in the daily averages for calorie intake. An important part of a healthy daily diet is water intake—approximately six twelve-ounce glasses per day. Drinking a glass of water with each meal is one way to help you fulfill that need. If you prefer other beverages with meals and snacks, such as coffee, tea, and soda, we recommend sugar-free varieties.

## Day 1

| | |
|---|---|
| **Breakfast** | 1 egg prepared without fat |
| | 1 slice toast with 1 tbsp peanut butter |
| | 1 fresh fruit |
| **Snack** | 1 stick mozzarella string cheese |
| **Lunch** | 4 oz grilled or baked chicken breast |
| | Salad with mixed greens and assorted raw vegetables |
| | 1 tbsp oil and vinegar dressing |
| **Snack** | 1 fresh fruit |
| **Dinner** | 4 oz baked fish fillet rubbed with olive oil, garlic, and other seasoning as desired |
| | 1 cup cooked green beans, seasoned as desired |
| | 1 medium broiled tomato sprinkled with Parmesan or goat cheese and other spices as desired |
| | 1 dinner roll |
| **Snack** | ½ cup instant pudding prepared with skim or low-fat milk |
| | 1 cup strawberries or ½ cup other berries |

## Day 2

| | |
|---|---|
| **Breakfast** | Smoothie |
| | Blend 6 oz silken tofu, ⅔ cup berries, 1 cup apple juice, 1 tsp vanilla, 1 small banana. |
| **Snack** | Raw veggies |
| **Lunch** | Tomato stuffed with tuna salad on a bed of greens |
| | To make tuna salad, combine 3 oz water-packed tuna, 1 hard-boiled egg, chopped, and 2 tbsp low-calorie mayonnaise. |
| **Snack** | 1 fresh fruit |
| **Dinner** | 1 serving Beef and Broccoli Sauté* |
| | ½ cup brown rice, steamed or cooked in water or broth |
| | Salad with mixed greens and assorted raw vegetables |
| | 2 tbsp oil and vinegar dressing |
| **Snack** | ½ cup sherbet |

---

### *Beef and Broccoli Saute (serves 4)

| | |
|---|---|
| ¾ lb lean beef strips | 5–6 cups broccoli pieces |
| 1 tbsp olive oil | 6 cloves minced garlic |
| 1 tsp sesame oil | 2 tbsp cooking sherry |
| 1 tbsp soy sauce | 1½ tbsp ginger root |
| ½ tsp red pepper flakes | |

Sauté garlic in olive oil, add other ingredients, and cook until meat is done and broccoli is al dente.

## Day 3

| | |
|---|---|
| **Breakfast** | 2 open-face turkey and cheese melts |
| | On each slice of bread, place a 1-oz slice turkey and 1 slice fat-free cheese. Broil until cheese is melted. |
| **Snack** | 2 large high-fiber crackers |
| | 1 slice low-fat cheese |
| **Lunch** | 1 serving Shredded Chicken Salad with Cranberries* served over mixed greens |
| **Snack** | ½ cup instant pudding made with skim or low-fat milk |
| **Dinner** | 4 oz roasted pork tenderloin |
| | ½ cup brown rice, steamed or cooked in water or broth |
| | 1 cup vegetable medley sauté |
| | Sauté a variety of fresh vegetables (e.g., peppers, onions, squash, snow peas) in olive oil and seasonings of your choice. |
| **Snack** | ½ cup fat-free frozen yogurt |

---

### *Shredded Chicken Salad with Cranberries (serves 4)

2 boneless chicken breasts, poached until meat falls apart

⅔ cup dried cranberries

3 celery stalks, diced

1 oz pecans, chopped

Shred poached chicken. Mix ingredients together, toss with dressing, and refrigerate 6–8 hours.

**Dressing:**

In a food processor, combine 2 egg yolks, 2 tbsp apple cider vinegar, 2 tsp sugar (or equivalent in sugar substitute), 1 tsp Dijon mustard. While blending, stream 2 tbsp olive oil into processor.

## Day 4

| | |
|---|---|
| **Breakfast** | 1 cup cereal with skim milk |
| | 1 fresh fruit |
| **Snack** | 2 lettuce and turkey wraps |
| | Wrap a 1-oz slice of turkey in each large lettuce leaf. |
| **Lunch** | Shrimp salad |
| | Serve 4 oz cooked shrimp with cocktail sauce and lemon juice on a bed of greens. |
| | 8 small low-fat crackers |
| **Snack** | ½ cup low-fat cottage cheese |
| | ½ cup fresh or canned pineapple in its own juice |
| **Dinner** | 1 roasted Cornish game hen, seasoned to taste |
| | 1 serving Braised Cauliflower with Capers* |
| | 1 medium baked sweet potato |
| **Snack** | 1 fresh fruit |

---

### *Braised Cauliflower with Capers (serves 4)

| | |
|---|---|
| 3 tbsp olive oil | 1 can anchovies, rinsed and minced |
| 3 garlic cloves | ¼ tsp dried red pepper flakes |
| 1 cup water | 1¼ lbs cauliflower florets |
| 3 tbsp capers | ¼ cup parsley, chopped |
| Salt to taste | |

Melt anchovies in olive oil over medium-low heat, about 1 minute. Add garlic and pepper flakes, cooking until garlic softens. Add cauliflower and water. Cover and cook 7 minutes or until tender. Remove lid; raise heat until water evaporates, leaving a thin layer of juice in bottom of pan. Add capers, parsley, salt, and serve.

## Day 5

| | |
|---|---|
| **Breakfast** | Omelet with 2 eggs with 1 oz nonfat cheese, 2 oz turkey, chopped green pepper, and mushrooms |
| | 1 fresh fruit |
| **Snack** | Raw veggies |
| **Lunch** | 1 cup low-fat, low-sodium soup (e.g., Healthy Choice, Campbell's Healthy Request) |
| | 8 small low-fat crackers |
| **Snack** | 1 fresh fruit |
| **Dinner** | Taco Salad in Baked Tortilla Bowl* |
| **Snack** | 1 fresh fruit |

---

### *Taco Salad in Baked Tortilla Bowl

| | |
|---|---|
| 4 oz lean ground beef | 1 tbsp taco spices |
| ½ chopped avocado | ½ chopped tomato |
| 2 tbsp sour cream | 1 oz shredded nonfat cheese |
| 1 whole-wheat tortilla | Mixed greens |

Line bottom and sides of ovenproof bowl with tortilla; bake at 350 degrees for 10–12 minutes. Cook beef with taco spices. Fill tortilla bowl with greens; top with meat, avocado, tomato, sour cream, and cheese. And you can eat the bowl!

---

---

# Day 6

| | |
|---|---|
| **Breakfast** | 1 cup cooked oatmeal with skim milk |
| | ¼ cup dried fruit or ½ sliced banana |
| **Snack** | 1 fresh fruit |
| **Lunch** | Turkey sandwich |
| | Place 4 oz turkey, 1 slice nonfat cheese, lettuce, and 1–2 tomato slices between 2 slices of bread. |
| | Raw veggies |
| | 1 oz pretzels |
| **Snack** | 6 oz low-sodium vegetable juice (e.g., V-8) |
| | 2 large high-fiber crackers (e.g., Ry Krisp) |
| **Dinner** | 4 oz chicken breast sautéed in olive oil and mixed herbs, such as pulverized basil, parsley, red pepper flakes, and salt |
| | ½ cup sautéed spinach with fresh garlic |
| | ½ cup brown rice, steamed or boiled in water or broth |
| **Snack** | ½ cup instant pudding made with skim or low-fat milk |

## Day 7

| | |
|---|---|
| **Breakfast** | 2 eggs |
| | 1 slice toast |
| **Snack** | 1 fresh fruit |
| **Lunch** | Chicken salad |
| | Toss together 4 oz white chicken meat, ¼ cup sliced grapes, 1 tbsp toasted chopped pecans, 1 tsp lemon juice, 1 tbsp fat-free plain yogurt. Serve on a bed of greens or wrapped in a large lettuce leaf. |
| **Snack** | 2 oz pretzels |
| **Dinner** | 4 oz baked or broiled salmon marinated in teriyaki sauce |
| | 1 cup vegetable medley sauté (see Day 3) |
| | ½ cup steamed or boiled brown rice, using water or broth |
| **Snack** | 1 fresh fruit |

# Day 8

| | |
|---|---|
| **Breakfast** | Smoothie (see Day 2) |
| **Snack** | 1 high-fiber granola or protein bar |
| **Lunch** | Salmon salad |
| | Toss together 3 oz leftover teriyaki salmon (or canned salmon), mixed greens, and 2 tbsp fat-free salad dressing. |
| **Snack** | 1 slice toast with 1 tbsp peanut butter |
| **Dinner** | 4 oz veal scallopini cooked in olive oil, lemon juice, and white wine, if desired |
| | 1 cup steamed asparagus with lemon juice |
| | Mixed green salad with ½ sliced tomato |
| | 2 tbsp vinaigrette salad dressing |
| **Snack** | 1 frozen fruit juice bar |

# Day 9

| | |
|---|---|
| **Breakfast** | 1 whole-wheat pita stuffed with 2 scrambled eggs and 2 oz nonfat shredded cheese |
| **Snack** | 1 fresh fruit |
| **Lunch** | 1 cup low-fat cottage cheese with ½ cup fresh or canned pineapple in its own juice |
| | 1 roll |
| **Snack** | 1 fresh fruit |
| **Dinner** | 1 serving Chicken Fajita Salad and Rice* |
| **Snack** | ½ cup sherbet |

---

### *Chicken Fajita Salad and Rice (serves 4)

| | |
|---|---|
| 1 lb chicken breast strips | Fajita (or taco) seasoning |
| 1 sliced onion | 1 sliced green pepper |
| 1 cup brown rice | 1 cup pico de gallo |

Marinate chicken strips 4–6 hours in seasoning. Make pico de gallo by mixing chopped onions, tomatoes, and cilantro with lemon juice and salt to taste.

Sauté marinated chicken strips with sliced onion and green pepper. Cook brown rice, adding a small amount of the seasoning to the water. Serve chicken mixture over rice, topped with pico de gallo.

---

## Day 10

| | |
|---|---|
| **Breakfast** | 1 cup cooked oatmeal with skim milk |
| | ¼ cup dried fruit, 1 cup strawberries, or ½ cup other berries |
| **Snack** | Raw veggies |
| **Lunch** | Tomato stuffed with tuna salad on a bed of greens (see Day 2) |
| **Snack** | 1 fresh fruit |
| **Dinner** | 4 oz grilled or baked fish fillet, seasoned to taste |
| | 1 cup fresh cooked green beans with slivered almonds |
| | Salad with mixed greens and assorted raw vegetables |
| | 2 tbsp oil and vinegar dressing |
| | 1 dinner roll |
| **Snack** | ½ cup sherbet |

---

## Day 11

---

**Breakfast**  Egg white omelet with 3 egg whites, 1 tbsp shredded fat-free cheese, and 1 tbsp meatless bacon bits

1 slice toast

**Snack**  1 stick mozzarella string cheese

**Lunch**  No-fat-added tuna salad

Toss together 3 oz water-packed tuna, ½ chopped tomato, 1 tbsp lemon juice, 1 tbsp chopped green onion, pinch of salt. Serve on a bed of greens or wrapped in a large lettuce leaf.

8 small low-fat crackers

**Snack**  Raw veggies

**Dinner**  4 oz grilled chicken breast marinated in Italian salad dressing

Whole baked tomato sprinkled with Parmesan or goat cheese

Spinach salad

Toss together 2 cups fresh spinach, ½ cup blueberries or ¼ cup raisins or other dried fruit, 1 tbsp Gorgonzola cheese, 1 tbsp toasted slivered almonds, and 2 tbsp vinaigrette salad dressing.

1 dinner roll

**Snack**  1 fresh fruit

---

# Day 12

---

| | |
|---|---|
| **Breakfast** | 1 cup cereal with skim milk |
| | ¼ cup dried fruit, 1 cup strawberries, or ½ cup other berries |
| | 6 oz low-sodium vegetable juice |
| **Snack** | 1 cup nonfat yogurt (plain or with fruit) |
| | ¼ cup low-fat crunchy cereal or granola |
| **Lunch** | 2 turkey roll-ups |
| | On a whole-wheat tortilla, spread 1 tbsp low-fat cream cheese, then place 2–3 spinach leaves, 2 oz sliced turkey, 4 thin cucumber slices. |
| **Snack** | 1 fresh fruit |
| **Dinner** | **Marinated and Grilled Flank Steak (serves 4)** |
| | Marinate (1–24 hours) 1 lb flank steak in ⅓ cup dry red cooking wine, ½ cup chopped sweet onion, 1 tbsp soy sauce, 3 cloves garlic, minced. Grill marinated meat to desired tenderness. |
| | 1 serving Corn and Black Bean Side* |
| | Salad with mixed greens and assorted raw vegetables |
| | 2 tbsp oil and vinegar dressing |
| **Snack** | ½ cup instant pudding made with skim or low-fat milk |

---

## *Corn and Black Bean Side (serves 4)

| | |
|---|---|
| ⅓ cup chopped red onion | 1 cup sweet corn, fresh or canned (drained) |
| 2–4 tbsp chopped cilantro | 1 cup canned black beans, drained and rinsed |
| 2–3 tbsp lemon juice | 1 cup chopped red pepper |

Mix together all ingredients. Serve chilled.

# Day 13

| | |
|---|---|
| **Breakfast** | 2 eggs |
| | 1 slice toast |
| | 1 fresh fruit |
| **Snack** | 8 small low-fat crackers |
| **Lunch** | Mixed green salad with assorted raw vegetables and leftover flank steak chunks or 3 oz turkey, chicken, or tuna |
| | 2 tbsp oil and vinegar dressing |
| **Snack** | 1 high-fiber granola or protein bar |
| **Dinner** | 4 oz fish fillet sautéed in trans-fat-free margarine and drizzled with lemon juice |
| | 1 cup vegetable medley sauté |
| | Sauté a variety of fresh vegetables (e.g., peppers, onions, squash, snow peas) in olive oil and seasonings of your choice. |
| | Green salad with assorted raw vegetables |
| | 2 tbsp oil and vinegar dressing |
| **Snack** | 1 fresh fruit |

## Day 14

| | |
|---|---|
| **Breakfast** | 1 cup cereal with skim milk |
| | 1 cup strawberries or 1 small banana |
| | 6 oz low-sodium vegetable juice |
| **Snack** | 1 fresh fruit |
| **Lunch** | Tuna salad sandwich |
| | Blend 3 oz water-packed tuna, chopped tomato and green onion as desired, 1 tsp lemon juice, 2 tbsp light mayonnaise; spread between 2 slices bread. |
| **Snack** | Raw veggies |
| **Dinner** | 4 oz beef tenderloin fillet, seasoned and grilled to taste |
| | ½ cup cooked green beans with slivered almonds |
| | 1 serving Fake-Out Mashed Potatoes* |
| **Snack** | 1 frozen fruit bar |

---

### *Fake-Out Mashed Potatoes (serves 4)

¼–½ cup skim milk  1 head cauliflower broken into florets

Butter substitute  Low-fat sour cream (optional)

Steam cauliflower until soft. Blend in food processor, adding milk until cauliflower reaches the consistency of mashed potatoes. Add butter substitute, salt, and pepper to taste. Serve with a dollop of low-fat sour cream if desired.

## Day 15

| | |
|---|---|
| **Breakfast** | 1 cup cereal with skim milk |
| | ¼ cup dried fruit, 1 cup strawberries, or 1 small sliced banana |
| **Snack** | ½ cup low-fat cottage cheese |
| | ½ cup diced pineapple, fresh or canned in its own juice |
| **Lunch** | Chicken Caesar salad with Parmesan cheese |
| | On a bed of romaine lettuce, layer 3 oz chunked white chicken, 1 tbsp Parmesan cheese, 2 tbsp Caesar salad dressing, 1 tbsp fat-free croutons. |
| **Snack** | 1 fresh fruit |
| **Dinner** | 4 oz roasted pork tenderloin, seasoned to taste |
| | 1 serving Baked Potato Wedges* |
| | ½ cup steamed snow peas with slivered almonds |
| **Snack** | ½ cup instant pudding made with skim or low-fat milk |

---

### *Baked Potato Wedges (serves 4)

Cut two large sweet potatoes lengthwise into wedges, skin on. Sprinkle with substitute butter, salt, and other spices (curry, tarragon, thyme) to taste. Bake 30 minutes at 375 degrees or until brown and cooked through.

# Day 16

| | |
|---|---|
| **Breakfast** | Smoothie (see Day 2) |
| **Snack** | 1 stick mozzarella string cheese |
| **Lunch** | 1 cup low-fat, low-sodium soup (e.g., Healthy Choice, Campbell's Healthy Request) |
| | 4 small low-fat crackers |
| | 1 slice low-fat cheese |
| **Snack** | Raw veggies |
| **Dinner** | 4 oz grilled chicken breast marinated in Italian salad dressing |
| | Whole baked tomato sprinkled with Parmesan or goat cheese |
| | Spinach salad |
| | Toss together 2 cups fresh spinach, ½ cup blueberries or ¼ cup raisins or other dried fruit, 1 tbsp Gorgonzola cheese, 1 tbsp toasted slivered almonds, and 2 tbsp vinaigrette salad dressing. |
| | 1 dinner roll |
| **Snack** | 1 fresh fruit |

## Day 17

| | |
|---|---|
| **Breakfast** | Omelet with 2 eggs, 1 oz nonfat cheese, 2 oz turkey, chopped green pepper, and mushrooms |
| | 1 fresh fruit |
| **Snack** | Raw veggies |
| **Lunch** | Chicken salad (see Day 7) |
| **Snack** | 1 fresh fruit |
| **Dinner** | Taco Salad in Baked Tortilla Bowl (see Day 5) |
| **Snack** | ½ cup instant pudding made with skim or low-fat milk |

## Day 18

| | |
|---|---|
| **Breakfast** | 1 cup cereal with skim milk |
| | 1 fresh fruit |
| **Snack** | 2 lettuce and turkey wraps (see Day 4) |
| **Lunch** | Shrimp salad (see Day 4) |
| | 8 small low-fat crackers |
| **Snack** | 1 fresh fruit |
| **Dinner** | 1 roasted Cornish game hen, seasoned to taste |
| | 1 serving Braised Cauliflower with Capers (see Day 4) |
| | 1 medium baked sweet potato, plain or with fat-free spread |
| **Snack** | 1 cup nonfat yogurt (plain or with fruit) |
| | ¼ cup low-fat crunchy cereal or granola |

## Day 19

| | |
|---|---|
| **Breakfast** | 1 cup cereal with skim milk |
| | ¼ cup dried fruit, 1 cup strawberries, or ½ cup other berries |
| | 6 oz low-sodium vegetable juice |
| **Snack** | Raw veggies |
| **Lunch** | Tomato stuffed with tuna salad on a bed of greens (see Day 2) |
| **Snack** | 1 fresh fruit |
| **Dinner** | 1 serving Beef and Broccoli Sauté (see Day 2) |
| | ½ cup brown rice, steamed or cooked in water |
| | Salad with mixed greens and assorted raw vegetables |
| | 2 tbsp oil and vinegar dressing |
| **Snack** | ½ cup sherbet |

---

# Day 20

| | |
|---|---|
| **Breakfast** | 2 open-face turkey and cheese melts (see Day 3) |
| **Snack** | ½ cup low-fat cottage cheese |
| | ½ cup fresh or canned pineapple in its own juice |
| **Lunch** | 1 serving Shredded Chicken Salad with Cranberries (see Day 3) |
| **Snack** | 1 fresh fruit |
| **Dinner** | 4 oz roasted pork tenderloin |
| | ½ cup brown rice, steamed or cooked in water or broth |
| | 1 cup steamed broccoli florets |
| | ½ cup steamed or boiled carrot slices |
| **Snack** | ½ cup fat-free frozen yogurt |

---

## Day 21

---

| | |
|---|---|
| **Breakfast** | 2 eggs |
| | 1 slice toast |
| **Snack** | 1 fresh fruit |
| **Lunch** | No-fat-added tuna salad (see Day 11) |
| | 8 small low-fat crackers |
| **Snack** | 2 oz pretzels |
| **Dinner** | 4 oz baked or broiled salmon marinated in teriyaki sauce |
| | 1 cup vegetable medley sauté (see Day 3) |
| | ½ cup brown rice steamed or boiled in water or broth |
| **Snack** | 1 fresh fruit |

# 22

## Spiritual Energy In: 90 Days with God's Word

Bible passages you can "feed on"
during your 90-Day Challenge.

The following Bible passages, arranged into a 90-day reading plan, have been
selected to nurture and energize your spiritual heart during your 90-Day
Challenge. Each day, enter the reference for the passage you read on your
Total Heart Health Journal page. As you read, be sensitive to what God is
saying to you and what He is telling you to do. Write your response in the
spaces provided on the journal sheet.

| | | |
|---|---|---|
| John 1:1–18 | 1 John 1:1–2:6 | Esther 2:1–23 |
| John 3:1–21 | 1 John 2:7–29 | Esther 3:1–15 |
| John 4:1–26 | 1 John 3:1–24 | Esther 4:1–17 |
| Psalms 1:1–6; 150:1–6 | 1 John 4:1–21 | Esther 5:1–14 |
| Ruth 1:1–22 | 1 John 5:1–21 | Esther 6:1–14 |
| Ruth 2:1–23 | 1 Corinthians 13:1–13 | Esther 7:1–10 |
| Ruth 3:1–18 | Matthew 5:1–20 | Esther 8:1–17 |
| Ruth 4:1–22 | Matthew 5:21–48 | Esther 9:1–19 |
| John 10:1–21 | Matthew 6:11–18 | Esther 9:20–10:3 |
| Psalms 23:1–6; 100:1–5 | Matthew 6:19–34 | Psalm 34:1–22 |
| Philippians 1:1–30 | Matthew 7:1–28 | James 1:1–27 |
| Philippians 2:1–30 | Ephesians 1:1–23 | James 2:1–26 |
| Philippians 3:1–21 | Ephesians 2:1–22 | James 3:1–18 |
| Philippians 4:1–23 | Ephesians 3:1–21 | James 4:1–17 |
| Psalm 103:1–22 | Ephesians 4:1–32 | James 5:1–20 |
| Hebrews 11:1–22 | Ephesians 5:1–33 | Psalm 51:1–19 |
| Hebrews 11:23–40 | Ephesians 6:1–24 | Matthew 13:1–30 |
| Hebrews 12:1–17 | Isaiah 53:1–12 | Matthew 13:31–58 |
| Psalm 37:1–22 | Romans 5:1–21 | Psalm 19:1–14 |
| Psalm 37:23–40 | Esther 1:1–22 | Romans 8:1–17 |

| | | |
|---|---|---|
| Romans 8:18–39 | Ecclesiastes 3:1–15 | Romans 14:1–23 |
| Psalm 139:1–24 | John 14:1–21 | Galatians 5:1–15 |
| John 12:1–11 | John 15:1–27 | Galatians 5:16–26 |
| 1 Peter 1:1–12 | Psalm 8:1–9 | Psalm 96:1–13 |
| 1 Peter 1:13–25 | Romans 12:1–21 | Matthew 18:1–20 |
| 1 Peter 2:1–12 | Psalm 95:1–11 | Matthew 18:21–35 |
| 1 Peter 2:13–25 | Colossians 1:1–29 | Matthew 25:1–13 |
| 1 Peter 3:1–22 | Colossians 2:1–23 | Matthew 25:14–30 |
| 1 Peter 4:1–19 | Colossians 3:1–25 | Matthew 25:31–46 |
| 1 Peter 5:1–13 | Colossians 4:1–18 | Proverbs 31:10–31 |

# NOTES

## Chapter 1: The Heart of the Matter

1. Bureau of Labor Statistics, "Labor Force Participation Rates, 1975–2008," http://stats.bls.gov/opub/working/data/chart3.txt (accessed April 1, 2005).

## Chapter 2: The Wonder of a Woman's Heart

1. Kerby Anderson, "Health and Church Attendance," Probe Ministries, www.probe.org/docs/c-health2.html (accessed August 28, 2004).

## Chapter 3: What's So Special About Your Heart?

1. S. Hully, *Journal of the American Medical Association* 280 (1998): 605 (HERS trial). D. M. Herrington, ERA trial, *New England Journal of Medicine* 343 (2000): 522 (ERA trial). Writing Group for Women's Health Initiative, *Journal of the American Medical Association* 288 (2002): 321. Writing Group for Women's Health Initiative, *Journal of the American Medical Association* 291 (2004): 1701.

## Chapter 5: Your Heart Is a Target

1. Rick Warren, *The Purpose Driven Life* (Grand Rapids: Zondervan, 2002), 23.

## Chapter 6: Heart Health: A Real Life and Death Matter

1. American Heart Association, http://www.americanheart.org (accessed August 28, 2004).

2. The Gallup Organization, Gallup survey, 1995. Adapted from the American Heart Association, *1999 Heart and Stroke Statistical Update* (1998):175.

3. National Center for Health Statistics, *Vital Statistics of the United States*, vol. 2— Mortality, Part A, 1992. Miller et. al., eds., *SEER Cancer Statistics Review 1973–1993*, National Cancer Institute.

4. American Heart Association, *1999 Heart and Stroke Statistical Update* (1993): 4.

5. Ibid., (1998): 4.

6. American Heart Association, *2003 Heart and Stroke Statistical Update* (2002): 4

7. Ibid.

8. Ibid., 12.

9. *Social Science & Medicine* 52 (2001): 1565; *Journal of the American Medical Association* 281 (1999): 901; *American Journal of Respiratory and Critical Care Medicine* (1998): 175.

10. *Circulation* 108 (2003): 2619–23.

11. J. Herlitz et al., "Mortality Risk Indications of Death, Mode of Death and Symptoms of Angina Pectoris During 5 Years After Coronary Bypass Grafting in Men and Women," *Journal of Internal Medicine* 247 (2000): 500–506.

12. V. Vaccarino et al., "Sex Differences in Hospital Mortality After Coronary Artery Bypass Surgery: Evidence for a Higher Mortality in Younger Women," *Circulation* 105 (2002): 1176–81. G. Christakis et al., "Is Body Size the Cause of Poor Outcomes of Coronary Artery Bypass Operations in Women?" *Journal of Thoracic and Cardiovascular Surgery* 110 (1995): 1344–58. L. Fisher et al., "Association of Sex, Physical Size and Operative Mortality After Coronary Artery Bypass in Coronary Artery Surgery (CASS)," *Journal of Thoracic and Cardiovascular Surgery* 84 (1982): 334–41. F. Edwards et al., "Impact of Gender on Coronary Bypass Operative Mortality," *Annals of Thoracic Surgery* 66 (1998): 125–312.

13. *Circulation* 108 (2003): 2619–23.

## Chapter 8: Are You Eating to Live or Living to Eat?

1. "AOA Fast Facts: What Is Obesity?" American Obesity Association, www.obesity.org (accessed September 16, 2004).

2. "AOA Facts Sheet: Obesity in the U.S.," American Obesity Association, www.obesity.org (accessed September 16, 2004).

3. Centers for Disease Control, National Center for Health Statistics, National Health and Nutrition Examination Survey, "Health, United States" (Table 70), 2002.

4. Ibid.

5. Ibid.

6. "What Is Obesity?" American Obesity Association, www.obesity.org.

7. Walter C. Willett, MD, *Eat, Drink, and Be Healthy: The Harvard Medical School Guide to Healthy Eating* (New York: Free Press, 2001).

## Chapter 9: Calories: Are They Friend or Foe?

1. National Weight Control Registry, www.nwcr.com (accessed August 28, 2004).

2. M. L. Klem, R. R. Wing, M. T. McGuire, H. M. Seagle, and J. O. Hill, "A Descriptive Study of Individuals Successful at Long-Term Maintenance of Substantial Weight Loss," *American Journal of Clinical Nutrition* 66 (1977): 239–46.

## Chapter 11: Five Fears That Will Erode Your Faith

1. Neil T. Anderson, Terry E. Zuehlke, and Julianne S. Zuehlke, *Christ Centered Therapy* (Grand Rapids: Zondervan, 2000), 42–43.

2. "Faith Speeds Recovery from Depression," http://www.mercola.com/1998/archive/faith_speeds_recovery_from_depresson.htm (accessed September 11, 2004).

3. "Spirituality Cuts Mortality Risk," http://www.mercola.com/1998/archive/spirituality.htm (accessed September 11, 2004).

4. Ibid.

5. Ibid.

6. "Faith Speeds Recovery from Depression."

7. "The Most Important Emotional Needs," http://www.marriagebuilders.com/graphic/mbi3300_needs.html (accessed September 14, 2004).

8. "Most Women 'Hate Their Bodies,'" http://news.bbc.co.uk/1/hi/uk/3206236.stm (accessed September 14, 2004).

## Chapter 13: Energy from the Proper Fuels

1. A. Ascherio, M. B. Katan, P. L. Zock, M. J. Stamphfer, and W. C. Willett, "Trans Fatty Acids and Coronary Heart Disease," *New England Journal of Medicine* 340 (1999): 1994–98.

2. F. B. Hu, L. Bronner, W. C. Willett, et al., "Fish and Omega 3 Fatty Acid Intake and Risk of Coronary Heart Disease in Women," *Journal of the American Medical Association* 287 (2002): 1815–21.

3. C. M. Albert, H. Campos, M. J. Stampfer, et al., "Blood Levels of Long-Chain n-3 Fatty Acids and the Risk of Sudden Death," *New England Journal of Medicine* 346 (2002): 1113–18.

4. "Early Protection Against Sudden Death by n-3 Polyunsaturated Fatty Acids After Miocardial Infarction: Time-Course Analysis of the Results of the GISSI Prevensione," *Circulation* 105 (2002): 1897–1903.

## Chapter 14: Adding Fire to Dietary Fuels

1. Eugene Braunwald, Anthony S. Fauci, Dennis L. Kasper, Stephen L. Hauser, Dan L. Longo, J. Larry Jameson, eds., *Harrison's Principles of Internal Medicine,* 14th ed. (New York: McGraw-Hill, 1998), 446.

## Chapter 15: Spiritual Energy for Every Hour of the Day

1. http://www.harvestprayer.com/pray101/pmen.html (accessed September 5, 2004).

2. http://www.reviveourhearts.com/radio/today/23629 (accessed September 5, 2004).

3. http://www.harvestprayer.com/pray101/pmen.html (accessed September 5, 2004).

4. http://www.news.harvard.edu/gazette/2004/05.13/01-prayer.html (accessed September 5, 2004).

## Chapter 16: Heart Exercise for Fun and Personal Profit

1. http://www.thefitmap.com/women/features/osteoporosis_and_exercise.htm (accessed September 2, 2004).

## Chapter 17: Are You Getting Daily Spiritual Workouts?

1. Rick Warren, *The Purpose Driven Life* (Grand Rapids: Zondervan, 2002), 283–84.

2. Antonio Porchia, *Voices* (Port Townsend, Wash.: Copper Canyon Press, 2003), 91.

## Chapter 18: Be Your Own Diet Guru

1. "Comparison of the Atkins, Ornish, Weight Watchers, and Zone Diets for Weight Loss and Heart Disease Risk Reduction—a Randomized Trial," *Journal of the American Medical Association* 293 (2005): 43–53.

2. http://www.health.gov/dietaryguidelines/dga2005/report (accessed September 14, 2004).

## Chapter 19: Get Your Guidance from the Guardian of Your Heart

1. Patricia Sellers, "The Business of Being Oprah," *Fortune*, April 1, 2002.

2. Marianne Williamson, *A Woman's Worth* (New York: Ballantine, 1993).

3. "Religious Movements Homepage: Deepak Chopra," http://religiousmovements.lib.virginia.edu/nrms/Chopra.html (accessed September 23, 2004).

4. *Utne Reader*, January–February 1995, http://religiousmovements.lib.virginia.edu/nrms/Chopra.html (accessed September 22, 2004)

5. Gary Zukav, *The Seat of the Soul* (New York: Fireside, 1989), 27–31.

6. Ibid., 37.

7. Iyanla Vanzant, *The Value in the Valley*, Mobipocket eBooks. Quoted in http://voices.cla.umn.edu/newsite/authors/VANZANTiyanla.htm (accessed September 22, 2004).

8. While documentation has not been found of Chesterton's response, the American Chesterton Society assumes that it actually happened. See http://www.chesterton.org/qmeister2/wrongtoday.htm.

9. Amy Wellborn, "The Feel-Good Spirituality of Oprah," *Our Sunday Visitor* (January 13, 2002), http://www.osv.com/periodicals/show-article.asp?pid=645 (accessed April 3, 2005).

## Chapter 20: Are You Ready for the 90-Day Challenge?

1. The Cooper Institute, "How People Change: Psychological Theories & the Transtheoretical Model for Behavioral Change," 2003.

2. For a detailed plan of action and journal, get *The Total Heart Health for Women Workbook* (Nashville: W Publishing, 2005).

3. For additional Bible reading and meditation resources, purchase *The Total Heart Health Devotional Guide* (Nashville: W Publishing, 2005). This is a devotional guide for each day of the year, complete with practical tips for spiritual and physical heart health.

## Chapter 21: Physical Energy In: Menus and Recipes

1. P. M. Kris-Etherton, W. S. Harris, and L. J. Appel, "Omega-3 Fatty Acids and Cardiovascular Disease. New Recommendations from the American Heart Association," *Arteriosclerosis, Thrombosis, and Vascular Biology* 23 (2003): 151–52.

# A New You in **90** Days

Ed and JoBeth Young of the Second Baptist Church of Houston, along with two of the nation's leading cardiologists, Michael Duncan and Richard Leachman, have developed the Total Heart Health system, a program that insures you keep a balanced focus on your physical and spiritual health with:

◆ Fitness Tips

◆ Smart Recipes

◆ Daily Devotions

◆ Tools to become your own health & fitness coach

◆ A 90-Day Total Heart Health Challenge

◆ All around strategies for better living

**www.thomasnelson.com**

NELSON IMPACT

W PUBLISHING GROUP

COUNTRYMAN

**TOTAL HEART HEALTH FOR WOMEN**
Hardcover • 0-8499-0012-3 • $22.99

**TOTAL HEART HEALTH FOR MEN**
Hardcover • 0-8499-0013-1 • $22.99

TOTAL HEART HEALTH
FOR WOMEN
WORKBOOK
**Tradepaper**
1-4185-0127-1
$16.99

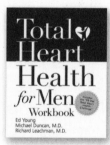

TOTAL HEART HEALTH
FOR MEN
WORKBOOK
**Tradepaper**
1-4185-0126-3
$16.99

365 DAYS OF
TOTAL HEART HEALTH
DEVOTIONAL
**Hardcover**
1-4041-0209-4
$15.99

TOTAL HEART HEALTH
POCKET PLANNER
**Tradepaper***
0-8499-9862-X

*FREE with book purchase

# Honor Christ Physically and Spiritually...
## with your **Total Heart**